T. JEFF.

"HARMONY in the married state is the very 1st object to be aimed at. Happiness by the domestic fireside is the 1st boon of heaven."

"To compel a man to furnish contributions of money for the propagation of opinions which he disbelieves is sinful & tyrannical."

"If we can prevent govt. from wasting the labors of the people under the pretense of taking care of them — they must become happy."

"The boys of the rising generation are to be the men of the next & the sole guardians of the principles we deliver over to them."

"A character of good faith is of as much value to a nation as to an individual. The moral obligations constitutes the law of nations as well as individuals."

"The policy of the Am. govt. is to leave their citizens free, neither restraining nor aiding them in their pursuits."

"State a moral case to a plowman and a Professor. The former will decide it as well & often better because he has not been led astray by any artificial rules."

"It is in the natural course of events that liberty recedes & govt. grows."

"I place ec. among the 1st & most important virtues, and pub. debt as the greatest of the dangers to be feared. We must make our election between ec. & liberty or profusion & servitude."

"I never considered a dif. of opinion in pol's in religion, in phil. as cause for withdrawing from a friend."

"The last hope of human liberty in the world rests on us. Our liberty cannot be guarded but by the freedom of the press."

"The bulk of mankind are school boys through life. Ed. is the true corrective of abuses of const. power."

"If we let Wash. tell us when to sow & when to reap the Nation shall soon want for bread."

THE NOTES

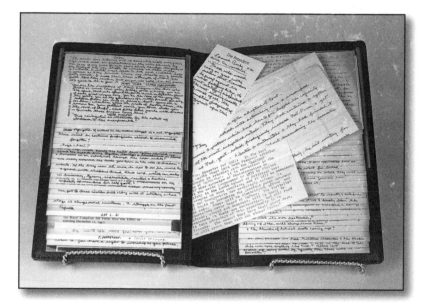

THE NOTES

Ronald Reagan's Private Collection

of Stories and Wisdom

EDITED BY DOUGLAS BRINKLEY

HARPER
An Imprint of HarperCollins*Publishers*
www.harpercollins.com

FIRST EDITION

Designed by William Ruoto

Library of Congress Cataloging-in-Publication Data
Reagan, Ronald.
   The notes : Ronald Reagan's private collection of stories and wisdom / by Ronald Reagan.
      p.   cm.
   ISBN 978-0-06-206513-1 (hardback)
   1. Reagan, Ronald—Quotations. 2. Reagan, Ronald—Humor. 3. American wit and humor. I. Title.
E838.5.R432   2011
081—dc22   2011008171

11 12 13 14 15   OV/RRD   10 9 8 7 6 5 4 3 2 1

*To all the men and women who
worked with Ronald Reagan in both
state and federal government*

CONTENTS

CONTENTS

INTRODUCTION

At the Reagan Presidential Library in Simi Valley, California, it's known as the Rosetta stone—the secret collection of 4-by-6 note cards on which our fortieth U.S. president recorded his favorite aphorisms, jokes, asides, and timeless nuggets of political wisdom. Although White House speechwriters such as Peggy Noonan, Ken Khachigian, and Tony Dolan had *heard* about Reagan's private notes collection, even occasionally witnessing him snatching an appropriate note out of his Oval Office desk drawer to insert into a speech draft, no one except Nancy Reagan had ever seen the full assemblage. Just as the fact that Reagan kept a daily diary as U.S. president from 1981 to 1989 surprised most people, the publication of *The Notes* is an equally important landmark event in Reagan studies. Anyone wondering about how Reagan—dubbed "The Great Communicator"—delivered such oratorical magic as a dinner speaker and itinerant statesman should read this compilation. These notes reveal the *real* Reagan—a fiercely patriotic, pro-democracy avatar of limited government.

It's believed that Reagan started *The Notes* collection when he was serving as a spokesperson for General Electric, from 1954 to 1962. Compelled to deliver hundreds of upbeat speeches a year to the Fortune 500 company's far-flung employees, Reagan devised a pragmatic method of keeping his hour-long public presentations both high-minded and lighthearted. A consummate showman, Reagan always padded salient contemporary political points with a couple of Borscht Belt one-liners followed by a wallop of engraved truth from one of the Founding Fathers. All those optimistic Eisenhower-era speeches focused on the virtues of free-market capitalism over Sovietism. Reagan listened, before and after speeches, to GE workers complain about high taxation and unnecessary regulations. He assimilated many of their sentiments into his own.

The backstory of how *The Notes* were rediscovered in 2010 is endearing. Under the direction of former First Lady Nancy Reagan, the library was getting a face-lift in time for the centennial of her husband's birth (February 6, 2011). Fifteen million dollars was raised to renovate from top to bottom the 26,000 square feet of the original exhibit space in the museum. Reagan Foundation executive director John Heubusch issued a clear directive: Let's find some exciting, new artifacts to put on museum display. The foundation's chief administrative officer and former Reagan aide Joanne Drake launched a hybrid treasure hunt–inventory to uncover hidden heirlooms—no easy task, given the sheer bulk of boxes deposited at the Reagan Library.

One afternoon in the spring of 2010, *The Notes*, published here, were discovered in a cardboard box marked only in pen with "RR's desk" on its side. There was no label on it. It was randomly stashed among boxes of assorted Reagan memorabilia. What a Eureka moment. Here were the personal belongings Reagan had kept in his office desk right up until his death in 2004. No one but Reagan himself probably ever recognized the historic value of these treasured notes, which he kept among a mass of rubber bands and paperclips. About 95 percent of the Reagan Library archive belongs to the U.S. federal government. The remaining 5 percent of material is the property of the Reagan Foundation. This amazing box of handwritten Reagan leavings—personal property owned by the former president—belongs to the foundation. A decision was soon made by the foundation to publish *The Notes*.

All of *The Notes* were handwritten. When Reagan was recopying various quotations he was especially neat. His scrawl is impeccable—seldom does he employ a cross-out or correct a mis-start. Clearly, legibility was a high priority to him. Sometimes he uses an asterisk or makes a hearty underline for emphasis. Shorthand is often the order of the day. The reader gets the impression that Reagan is a redwood tree and these are the decorations of his own philosophy, the ammunition he will need to survive the hustings ahead.

In addition to admiring the former president's penmanship, those who analyzed *The Notes* made some preliminary historical assessment. The notes that are published in this volume under the heading "Humor" are one-liners that were maintained in a fat stack of cards with a rubber band around them. They were separate from the rest of the collection. Whenever Reagan heard or invented a joke that he deemed a "keeper," he'd carefully write it out on a 4-by-6 note card and insert it in this stack. All the other axioms and aphorisms in this volume—all written in his own hand and found under the rubrics "On the Nation," "On Liberty," "On War," "On the People," "On Religion," "The World," "On Character," and "On Political Theater"—were kept in the plastic sleeves of a black photo album. There was no categorical arrangement of the notecards under headings. I devised that method to make it easier for the reader. This album artifact, the notecards yellowed around the edges, is now on permanent display at the renovated Reagan Library, unveiled as part of the 2011 centennial celebration.

Longtime friends of Reagan's remember that sometimes when he delivered a speech he'd throw the card of a joke that fell flat or of a nugget of political wisdom that tanked in front of an audience's ears into a wastepaper basket. What made it into the photo album were his golden oldies, his trench-tested winners, the intellectual ideas of notable others that best reflected his own worldview. At the collection's core is Reagan's bedrock belief that freedom and liberty come with the cost of being an alert and well-informed citizen. The collection constitutes a love song to America, the backbone of his most cherished ideas.

Many of the one-liners, jokes, high wisdom, straight talk, and political aphorisms in *The Notes* were delivered at one time or another in a public forum. If Reagan had one artifact that he would have saved were his house on fire, it would probably have been his card-stuffed photo album.

Its contents were tools of his trade as GE spokesperson, roast master, California governor, and U.S. president. There are hundreds of Thomas Jefferson quotes, for example, that are regularly offered up by U.S. politicians at rubber-chicken dinners and in stump speeches. What is interesting is why Reagan gravitated toward the handful of Jefferson in this volume. It's his *choices* that are fascinating.

The reason the Reagan Library calls *The Notes* a Rosetta stone is that the general public can easily deconstruct from this collection Reagan's own political philosophy. There is a gravitas to the quotes he chose to save in his private album. With the exception of the one-liners, all the collected wisdom in *The Notes* constitutes Reagan's Greatest Hits. And there are some shockers—who ever thought Reagan would have found anything useful from Mao or Norman Thomas? Even Reagan's political adversaries in America, like George McGovern, Walter Mondale, and Pat Brown, conceded that the Gipper's great gift was an innate ability to deliver a pitch-perfect joke, put-down, or ice-breaking one-liner on cue. When Robert F. Kennedy debated Reagan in 1967 about the Vietnam War—and Kennedy lost—Kennedy recognized that his rival had honed his gladiatorial routine to utter perfection, with an acute sense of timing, aw-shucks nods, chuckles, and eye rolls. "Reagan," RFK concluded, "was the toughest debater I ever went up against."

Part of Reagan's political success was the shrewd incorporation of the *Bartlett's Book of Quotations*–like truisms found in this volume. While others thought Reagan was a conservative revolutionary, our fortieth president knew that he was speaking in the same vein as Washington, Lincoln, Paine, and FDR. Books like John Stuart Mill's *On Liberty* and Adam Smith's *The Wealth of Nations* infused Reagan with genuine intellectual excitement, a collected wellspring of acumen.

It's important for readers to understand that *The Notes* is composed of raw, unedited primary source documents. Reagan, for example, quotes the historian Arnold Toynbee as having written, "Hist. is the pattern of silken slippers descending the stairs & thunder of hobnail boots coming." This quote is, in fact, a paraphrase of Voltaire. But Reagan learned it secondhand from Toynbee; therefore Toynbee receives the attribution. There are a number of examples like this in *The Notes*. Taken collectively, the notes in this book form a raw primary source document.

About 40 percent of *The Notes* published here were written on White House cards. The others were on the personal stationery cards he used as governor of California. It's thought that others date back to his GE years in the 1950s—survivors from the lecture circuit that he brought with him to his Oval Office desk. Only a handful of the quotes and jokes weren't handwritten on the 4-by-6 cards. A few rogue ones were penned on irregularly shaped cards, which he clearly scribbled down on the run.

Around the time *The Notes* were discovered in Simi Valley, an archivist also found boxes of handwritten and typed speeches on more cards from Reagan's years as governor, between 1967 and 1975. An ambitious Reagan historian of the future can write a fine scholarly paper mixing and matching the roles the note cards played in these varied high-profile speeches. Over the years I got to know a lot of old Reagan hands, ranging from Martin Anderson to George Bush, James Baker to Michael Deaver and Paul Laxalt. All of them used to collect good jokes to share with Reagan, as if pursuing a hobby. As speechwriter Aram Bakshian noted, "I used to spend a lot of time writing funny lines in the President's speeches. Then I'd see them taken out by the President in favor of better lines that he would add." Those fresh infusions of humor came from his note card collection.

What has become clear to me since I first wrote about Reagan in *The New Yorker* back in 1999 is that the former president had a communications system all his own. He controlled his own game. He was always his own man. The photo album was how he kept his most essential reference material. Because we know Reagan discarded many cards over the decades, we should consider this collection his pruned and manicured game book. It must have been a nice feeling to have Jefferson, Hamilton, and even Thomas Wolfe in your arsenal. For if Reagan is remembered as the Great Communicator, these notes provide the most effective way of decoding how he perfected his craft. As a historical document, *The Notes* showcases Reagan as one of the wittiest residents of the 1600 Pennsylvania Avenue address. It becomes obvious that he found solace from both predecessors and contemporaries who had something memorable to say that reinforced his own Main Street values.

NOVEMBER 17, 2010
HOUSTON, TEXAS

ON THE
NATION

⇥ John Stuart Mill & Daniel Webster

The Pres. has ltd. power. He may err without causing great mischief to the state. Cong. may decide amiss without destroying the union because the people may retract their decision by changing the members. But if the Sup. Ct. is ever compounded of imprudent men the Union may be plunged into anarchy or civil war.

⤳❦⤶

The Despotism America will face will degrade even men without tormenting them. Above this race of men will stand an immense and tutelary power which takes upon itself alone to secure man's gratifications and to watch over their fate. The power which this govt. shall exert shall be absolute, minute, regular, prudent & mild. For the happiness of this race of men such a govt. willingly labors. But in return it elects to be their sole agent and the only arbiter of their happiness. The govt. provides for this race security, it foresees & supplies their necessities, facilitates their pleasures, manages their prim. concerns, directs their industry, regulates the descent of their property and sub divides their inheritance. What can remain for this races govt. but to spare them the care of thinking and the trouble of living. Thus through its regulations—

⤛⤜

Nothing will ruin the country if the people themselves will undertake its safety; and nothing can save it if they leave that safety in any hand but their own.

⤛⤜

But who shall reconstruct the fabric of demolished govt. Who shall rear again the well proportioned cols. of constitutional lib. Who shall frame together the skillful architecture which unites nat. sovereignty with states rts. individ. security & pub. prosperity.

⤛⤜

Hold on to the constitution of the U.S. of Am. & to the Rep. for which it stands. Miracles do not cluster what has happened once in 6000 yrs. may never happen again. Hold on to your const. for if the Am. Const. shall fall there will be anarchy throughout the world.

⊰⊱ Alexis de Tocqueville

It sometimes happens in a people among whom various opinions prevail that the balance of parties is lost & one of them obtains an irresistible preponderance, overpowers all obstacles, annihilates its opponents & the vanquished despair of success, hide their heads and are silent. (Detoc. explaining the disappearance of the Fed. Party in the 1820's)

⤖

Dem. will last until the people in power learn they can perpetuate themselves in power through taxation.

⇥ Francis Lieber (Prof. U Columbia
   [1859] "On Civil Lib & Self Govt.")

Woe to the country in which pol. hypocrisy first calls
the people almighty, then teaches that the voice of the
people is divine, then pretends to take a mere clamor
for the true voice of the people & lastly gets up the
desired clamor. (Getting up the desired clamor is what
we call rocket engineering)

⇥ John Winthrop, Deck of Arbella, 1630,
   off Massachusetts Coast

We shall be as a city upon a hill. The eyes of all people
are upon us, so that if we shall deal falsely with our
God in this work we have undertaken & so cause him
to withdraw his present help from us, we shall be made
a story & a byword throughout the world.

✒ Whittaker Chambers

It is idle to speak of saving western civ. because western civ. is already a wreck from within. That is why we can hope to do little more now than snatch a fingernail of a saint from the rock or a handful of ashes from the fagots, & bury them secretly in a flower point against the day, ages hence, when a few men begin again to dare to believe that there was once something else, that something else is thinkable & need some evidence of what it was & the fortifying knowledge that there were those who at the great nitefall, took loving thought to preserve the tokens of hope & truth.

✒ Former P.M.—Australia

I wonder if anybody has thought what the situation of the comparatively small nat's. of the world would be if there were not in existence the U.S.—if there were not this giant country prepared to make so many sacrifices.

⇥ Letter by Samuel Adams (1789)

I have always been apprehensive that through the weakness of the human mind often discovered even in the wisest & best of men, or the perverseness of the interested & designing, in as well as out of govt., misconstruction would be given to the Fed. Const.— hazard the liberty, independence & happiness of the people—would gradually, but swiftly & imperceptibly run into a consolidated govt. pervading & legislating through all the States, not for federal purposes only as it professes, but in all cases whatsoever. Such a govt. would soon totally annihilate the Sovereignty of the several states not necessary to the support of the confederated Commonwealth, & sink both in despotism.

⇥ Anonymous

Too many Americans today have little or no faith in Social Freedom. They put their trust in govt. as the distributor of material goods preferring laws passed by their legislators to the works of the mkt. place.

❧ Sen. Fulbright at Stanford U.

The Pres. is our moral teacher & our leader he should be freed from the shackles of ill informed pub. opinion. He is hobbled in his task by the restrictions of power imposed on him by a Const. system designed for an 18th century agrarian society.

❧ Henry Steele Commager, 1953

Only the Pres. because he is the chief exec. is in a position to know all the facts. Only the Pres. and his advisors are in a position to weigh all the facts. Therefore the Pres. alone can lead the country.

⇥ Alex Hamilton on Impeachment

The greatest danger is that the decision will be regulated more by the comparative strength of parties than by a real demonstration of innocence or guilt.

⇥ Thomas Jefferson

The germ of dissolution of our Fed. govt. is in the Fed. Judiciary, an irresponsible body working like gravity, gaining a little today & a little tomorrow, & advancing its noiseless step like a thief over the field of jurisdiction until all shall be usurped from the states & the govt. of all be consolidated into one.

⁓✦⁓

1813: The same pol. parties that agitate the U.S. have existed through all time. Whether the power of the people or of the elite should prevail were questions which kept the states of Greece & Rome in eternal convulsions.

∾∾∾

The policy of the Am. govt. is to leave their citizens free, neither restraining nor aiding them in their pursuits.

∾∾∾

A character of good faith is of as much value to a nation as to an individual. The moral obligations constitute the law of nations as well as individuals.

∾∾∾

I place ec. among the 1st & most important virtues and pub. debt as the greatest of the dangers to be feared.

We must make our election between ec. & liberty or profusion & servitude.

⚜

If we let Wash. tell us when to sow & when to reap the Nation shall soon want for bread.

⚜

A rebuke to Cong. "How could it be otherwise in a body to which the people send 150 lawyers whose trade it is to question everything, yield nothing & talk by the hour."

⚜

The basis of our govt. being the opinion of the people, the very 1st object should be to keep that right; & were it left to me to decide whether we should have govt. without newspapers or newspapers without govt., I should unhesitatingly prefer the latter.

⁓

Wise & frugal govt. which shall restrain men from injuring one another, which shall leave them otherwise free to regulate their own pursuits of industry & improvement & shall not take from the mouth of labor the bread it has earned.

⇥ Abe Lincoln

1864—By general law life & limb must be protected, yet often a limb must be amputated to save a life, but a life is never wisely given to save a limb. I felt that measures otherwise unconst. might become lawful by becoming indispensable to the preservation of the nation. Right or wrong I assumed that ground & now avow it.

⇥ Montesquieu, 1748—Forms of Govt.

Each has a special relationship to its people. When that relationship is changed that form of govt. is doomed. 1—Dictatorship—Fear (can't survive if people no longer fear the dictator). 2—Monarchy—respect & affection for the Crown. 3—Rep. Govt.—There must be virtue among the people.

⇥ Winston Churchill

Some people regard private enterprise as a predatory tiger to be shot. Others look on it as a cow they can milk. Not enough people see it as a healthy horse pulling a sturdy wagon.

⇥ Franklin Delano Roosevelt, 1935

The Fed. govt. must & shall quit this business of relief. Continued dependence upon relief induces a spiritual & moral disintegration fundamentally destructive to Nat. fibre. To dole out relief in this way is to administer a narcotic, a subtle destroyer of the human spirit.

⇥ F.D.R., Pittsburgh, Oct. 19, 1932

Most of this new govt. created credit has been taken to finance the govt.'s continuing deficits. The truth is that the burden is absorbing their resources. All this is highly undesirable & wholly unnecessary. It arises from one cause only and that is the unbalanced bud. and the continued failure of this admin. to take effective steps to balance it. If that budget had been fully & honestly balanced in 1930 as it could have been, some of the 1931 collapse would have been avoided. Even if it had been balanced in 1931 as it could have been, much of

the extreme dip in 1932 would have been obviated. . . .
Would it not be infinitely better to clear this whole
subject of obscurity—to present the facts squarely to
the Cong. and the people of the U.S. & secure the
one sound foundation of permanent econ. recovery—a
complete & honest balance of the Fed. Bud.?

⇥ John F. Kennedy Re: His Tax Cut

Our true choice is not between tax reduction on the
1 hand & the avoidance of large Fed. deficits on the
other. Our economy stifled by restrictive tax rates will
never produce enough revenue to balance the budget.
Just as it will never produce enough jobs or enough
profits.

ᐒ Woodrow Wilson

America is sauntering thru the mazes of pol.'s with easy nonchalance. But presently there will come a time when she'll be surprised to find herself grown old—a country crowded, strained, perplexed. When she will be obligated to fall back upon her conservatism—obliged to pull herself together, adopt a new regimen of life, husband her resources, concentrate her strength, steady her methods, sober her views, restrict her vagaries, trust her best, not her average members.

ᐒ Cicero

The budget should be balanced, the treasury should be refilled, the pub. debt should be reduced, the arrogance of officialdom should be tempered & controlled. Assistance to foreign lands should be curtailed lest Rome become bankrupt. The mob should be forced to work & not depend on govt. for sustenance.

⇥ F.D.R.

The doctrine of reg. & legis. by masterminds in whose judgment and will all the people may gladly & quietly acquiesce has been too glaringly apparent in Wash. Were it possible to find masterminds so unselfish, so willing to decide unhesitatingly against their own personal interest—such a govt. might be to the interest of the country but there are none such on the pol. horizon.

⇥ Frederic Bastiat Addressing Nat. Assembly—France, 12/12/1849

The govt. offers a cure for the ills of mankind. It promises to restore commerce, make agri. prosperous, expand industry, encourage arts & letters, wipe out poverty, etc. etc. All that is needed is to create some new govt. agencies & to pay a few more bureaucrats.

⇥ Bastiat

When a nation is burdened with taxes nothing is more difficult or impossible than to levy them equally. What is still more difficult however is to shift the tax burden onto the shoulders of the rich. The state can have an abundance of money only by taking from everyone especially from the masses.

⚜

The state is the fictitious entity by which everyone seeks to live at the expense of everyone else.

⚜

The state quickly understands the use of the role the pub entrusts to it. It will be the arbiter, the master of all destinies. It will take a great deal hence a great deal will remain for itself. It will multiply the number of its agents . . . it will end by acquiring overwhelming proportions.

⋺ **Robert M. Hutchins**

The American experiment of leaving ed. to 50 states & 40,000 school boards is drawing to a close. Fed. aid to education formally on a massive scale is inevitable & the sooner it comes the better.

⋺ **Leonard Read**

Inflation is a device for siphoning govt. property into the coffers of govt. Successful hedging would require finding a form of property that cannot be confiscated. It does not exist. Pare govt. back to size; that is the only way to protect private property against confiscation.

⤳ Arthur Krock "Memoirs"

As a Wash. eyewitness of governmental and other public action through the years I formed the opinion that the U.S. merits the dubious distinction of having discarded its past & its meaning in one of the briefest spans of modern hist. Among the changes are—fiscal solvency & confidence in a stable $ driven from the national & foreign mkt. place by continuous deficit spending, easy credit, & growing unfavorable balance of payments in the international ledger of the U.S.; the free enterprise system shackled by organized labor & a govt.-managed economy; the govt. transmuted into a [welfare] it subsidized from Wash. & spoiled generations young to old led to expect the govt. to provide for all their wants, free of any of the requirements of responsible citizenship.

⇥ Vladimir Lenin

The way to take over a country is to debauch the currency. Through a continuous policy of inflation a govt. can quietly & unobservedly confiscate the wealth of its citizens.

⇥ Calvin Coolidge

The Nat. which forgets its defenders will itself be forgotten.

⇥ Paul McCracken on Pub. Debt

If we carry the arithmetic of projected savings flows & probable financing in '75 to its logical end we arrive at the interesting conclusion that the savings stream might well fall some short of what will then be required for financing.

⚜

Economists traditionally have tended to ignore these financial questions, but pressure in the cap. mkts. during the last few years remind us about the need to bring together savings & investment or savers & borrowers in an orderly way through the cap. mkts.

⇥ Randolph E. Paul, Under Sec.— Treasury—"Taxation For Prosperity" p. 217

The point is that taxes may be imposed, wholly apart from the revenue-producing qualities, to achieve desired effects on particular occasions . . . On this higher level taxes may be used to express public policy on the distribution of wealth & income; progressive income & estate taxes perform this function. They may be used to subsidize or penalize particular industries and econ. groups.

⊰⊱ Late Sumner Slichter Hvd.

The tax hist. of the U.S. in recent years has been fairly sensational. A visitor from Mars would suspect that a communist 5th columnist was writing the laws for the purpose of making private enterprise unworkable.

⊰⊱ William Gladstone 100 Years after Our Constitution

I consider the const. to be the more remarkable political advance ever accomplished one time by the human intellect.

☙ Anonymous

When the courts sub. their will for that of the legis. appealing to what *ought* to be law when they can find no law & what ought to be the const. when that document itself gives not the slightest justification for asserting the new prin. then we have reached the end of the road.

☙ Will Rogers

We will never get anywhere with our finances till we pass a law saying that every time we appropriate something we got to pass another bill along with it stating where the money is coming from.

⊰ Nation Magazine Letter from Woman Who Fled Poland Before Martial Law

Among many of our American born friends it is not fashionable to be enthusiastic about Am. There is Vietnam, drugs, urban & racial conflict, poverty & pollution. Undoubtedly this country faces urgent & serious problems. But we newcomers see not only the problems but also democratic solutions being sought & applied. I love Am. because people accept me for what I am. They don't question my ancestry, my faith, my pol. beliefs. When I want to move from one place to another I don't have to ask permission. When I need a needle I go to the nearest store & get one. I don't have to stand in line for *hours* to buy a piece of tough fat meat. Even with inflation I don't have to pay a day's earnings for a small chicken. I love Am. because Am. trusts me. I don't have to show an identity card to buy a pair of shoes. My mail isn't censored, my phone isn't tapped, my conversation with friends isn't reported to the secret police.

⤨ Letter I Received from Cub Scout

I love America because you can join Cub Scouts if you want to. You have a right to worship as you please.

⤨ Mark Hawley, Seattle, Wash.

If you have the ability you can try to be anything you want to be. I also like Am. because we have about 200 flavors of ice cream.

≫ Ted Sorensen Decision in The White
House

Public opinion—often erratic, inconsistent, arbitrary
& unreasonable—frequently hampered by myths &
misinformation, by stereotypes & shibboleths & by
innate resistance to innovation—for these reasons Pres.
must not be bound by pub. opinion. He must reign in
Wash. but he must also rule.

ON LIBERTY

⧊ Thomas Wolfe

To every man his chance, to every man regardless of his birth his shining golden opportunity. To every man the right to live, to work, to be himself & to become whatever his manhood & his vision can combine to make him. This seeker is the promise of Am.

⇥ John Adams at Signing of Dec. Independence

Sink or swim, live or die, survive or perish, I give my hand and my heart to this vote. It is true that in the beginning we aimed not at independence. But there's a divinity that shapes our ends. I know the uncertainties of human affairs. But I see through this day's business. We may die, die as colonists; die as slaves; die it may be on the scaffold. Be it so. But while I live, let me have a country or at least the hope of a country, at least the hope of a country, and *that* a *free* country. But whatever be our fate, be assured, that this declaration will stand. . . . All that I have, and all that I am and all that I hope to be in life I am now ready to stake upon it; and I leave off as I began, that live or die, survive or perish, I am for the declaration.

⇥   Thomas Jefferson

If a nation expects to be *ignorant* & *free* in a state of civilization, it expects what never was & what never will be.

⚘

The last hope of human liberty in the world rests on us. Our liberty cannot be guarded but by the freedom of the press.

⇥   John Stuart Mill & Daniel Webster

If the roads, the railways, the banks, the insurance offices, the great joint stock companies, the U's and the family charities were all of them branches of the govt. If the emps. of all of these diff. enterprises were appt'd and pd. by the govt. and looked to the govt. for every ride in life; not all the freedom of the press and popular const. of the legis. would make this country free otherwise than in name.

⚜

A state which dwarfs its men in order that they may be more docile instruments in its hands—even for beneficial purposes—will find that with small men no great thing can really be accomplished.

⇥ Alexis De Tocqueville

The man who asks of freedom anything other than itself is born to be a slave.

⚜

It daily renders the exercise of the free agency of this race of man less useful & less frequent; this govt. grad. this race of man of all the uses of the individual man. This govt. has predisposed this race of man to endure these individually, small & petty erosions of individ. liberty & often to look upon them as benefits. It covers the whole surface of svc. with a network of small complicated rules. A network of individually uniform rules thru which the most orig. minds & most energetic characterize cannot penetrate to rise above the crowd. The will of man has not been shattered; it has been softened, bent and guided. Men are seldom forced to act, but are constantly prevented from acting. The Nat. is reduced to nothing better than a flock of timid & industrious animals & govt. is the shepherd.

⤐ Pope Pius 12th, End WWII

When I took up my little sling and aimed at communism I also hit something else. I hit the force of that great socialist revolution which under the name of liberalism spasmodically, incompletely & somewhat formlessly has been inching its ice cap over this nat. for 2 decades. Though I knew it existed, still I had no idea of its extent or the depth of its penetration or the fierce vindictiveness of its revolutionary temper—which was the reflex of its struggle to keep & advance its pol. power.

⤐ Anonymous

The real Am. idea is not that every man shall be on a level with every other, but that every man shall have the liberty without hindrance to be what God made him. The office of govt. is not to <u>confer</u> happiness but to give men the opp. to work out happiness for themselves.

⤐ Edmund Burke on The Threat of Socialism

A perfect equality will indeed be produced—that is to say equal wretchedness, equal beggary, and on the part of partitioners a woeful, helpless and desperate disappointment. Such is the event of all compulsory equalizations. They pull down what is above; they never raise what is below; they depress high & low together, beneath the level of what was originally the lowest.

⤐ Winston Churchill

Socialism is the phil. of failure, the creed of ignorance, the gospel of envy. Its inherent virtue is the equal sharing of misery.

⤝⤞

The inherent vice of capitalism is the unequal sharing of blessings while the inherent virtue of Soc. is the equal sharing of miseries.

⤝ On The Labor Party Prog. 1945

I do not believe in the power of the state to plan & enforce. No matter how numerous are the committees they set up, or the ever growing hordes of officials they employ, or the severity of the punishments they inflict or threaten, they cannot approach the high level of internal economic production achieved under free enterprise. Personal initiative, competitive selection, the profit motive, corrected by failure & the infinite processes of good housekeeping & personal ingenuity, these constitute the life of a free society. It is this vital creative impulse that I deeply fear the . . .

⇥ Woodrow Wilson

A revolution is taking place which will leave people dependent on govt. Finding mkts. will develop into fixing prices & finding employment. Next step will be to furnish employment or in default pay a bounty or dole. Those who look with apprehension on these tendencies do not lack humanity but are influenced by the belief that the result of such measures will be to deprive the people of character & liberty.

⚜

Liberty has never come *from* govt. The hist. of liberty is the hist. of limitation of govt. power not the increase of it.

⇥ Thomas Macaulay

Our rulers will best promote the improvement of the people by confining themselves to their own legit. duties—by leaving capital to find its most lucrative course, commodities their fair price, industry & intelligence their natural reward, idleness & folly their natural punishment; by diminishing the price of law, by maintaining peace, by defending property & observing strict economy in every dept. of the state. Let govt. do this—the people will assuredly do the rest.

⇥ Daniel Webster

Hold on my friends to the Constitution of the United States of America & to the Repub. for which it stands. Miracles do not cluster. What has happened once in 6000 yrs. may never happen again. Hold on to your const. for if the const. shall fall there will be anarchy throughout the world.

⇥ George Bernard Shaw

Socialism means equality of inc. or nothing. Under Soc. you would not be allowed to be poor. You would be forcibly fed, clothed, lodged, taught & employed whether you liked it or not. If it were discovered that you had no character or industry enough to be worth all this trouble, you might possibly be executed in a kindly manner, but while you were permitted to live you would have to live well.

⇥ Frederic Bastiat Addressing Nat. Assembly—France, 12/12/1849

Heavy govt. expenditures and liberty are incompatible. Woe to the people that cannot limit the sphere of action of the state. Freedom, private enterprise, wealth, happiness, independence, personal dignity—all vanish.

⇥ Calvin Coolidge, William & Mary, May 15, 1926

No method of procedure has ever been devised by which liberty could be divorced from local self govt. No plan of centralization has ever been adopted which did not result in bureaucracy, tyranny, reaction & decline of all forms of govt. those administered by bureaus are about the least satisfactory for an enlightened & progressive people. Being irresponsible they become autocratic & being autocratic they resist all development. Unless bureaucracy is constantly resisted it breaks down representative govt. & overwhelms democracy. It is the one element in our insts. that sets up a pretense of having authority over everybody & being responsible to nobody.

⇥ 1927, Rev. Rauschenbusch "New Leader," Official Soc. Paper

The Am. people will never knowingly stage a revolution to bring about socialism. So we should promote the idea by increasing govt. control of business & having Socialists get govt. jobs. one man in govt. with his eyes & ears open can do more than a hundred men on the outside. They must work to promote more govt. control of banks, R.R.'s, & other businesses; to start a program of govt. ownership of elec. power & to work for pol. control & management of all key industries. (It didn't bother the Rev. that people who wouldn't knowingly vote for Soc. should have it forced on them).

⇥ Samuel Gompers Last Speech Before Labor Convention

There may be here & there a worker who does not join a union of labor. That is his right no matter how wrong we think he may be. It is his legal right & no one can dare question his legal exercise of that right.

⚜

1924—Urged Fundamentals of Human Liberty: No lasting good has ever come from compulsion.

⚜ Statue of Liberty

Her name—Mother of Exiles. From her beacon hand glow world wide welcome; her mild eyes command the air bridged harbor that twin cities frame. Keep your ancient lands, your storied pomp; cries she with silent lips—Give me your tired, your poor, your huddled masses yearning to breathe free, the wretched refuse of your teeming shore. Send these, the homeless, tempest-tost to me. I lift my lamp beside the golden door.

The Notes

⇥ Louise E. Weber, "I Love This Land"

I may inhabit worlds in time to come of finer substance, born of further suns; a greater glory I may one day see, but oh today, dear earth, how I love thee.

⇥ Vladimir Lenin

Go to youth, form fighting squads everywhere. Let groups be organized of 3, 10, 30 persons. Let them arm themselves as best they can with a revolver, knife, rag soaked in kerosene for starting fires. Do not make membership in the party an absolute condition. That would be an absurd demand for an armed uprising. You must proceed with propaganda on a wide scale. Propagandists must supply each group with a brief & simple recipe for making bombs. Squads must begin military training. Some may undertake to kill, to spy or blow up police stations, others to raid the bank to confiscate money for the insurrection.

❦

Be prepared to resort to every illegal device to conceal the truth—It would not matter if ¾ of the human race perished; the important thing is that the remaining ¼ be communist.

❦

The communist party enters into Bourgeois insts. not to do constructive work but in order to direct the masses to destroy from within the whole Bourgeois state machine & the parliament itself.

⇥ Joseph Stalin

Words must have no relation to actions, otherwise what kind of diplomacy is it? Words are one thing, action another. Good words are a mask for concealment of deeds. Sincere diplomacy is no more possible than dry water or wooden iron.

⇥ Nikita Khrushchev

Despite the difference between the stages of comm. & soc. no wall of any kind exists between them . . . communism grows from soc. & its direct continuation.

⇥ Comm. Party U.S.A. Oath, 1930

I pledge myself to rally the masses to defend the Soviet U., the land of victorious socialism. I pledge myself to remain at all times a vigilant & firm defender of the Leninist line of the party, the only line that insures the triumph of Soviet power in the U.S.

✥ Nazi Party on What Should Be Party Platform

Demand that the state shall make one of its chief duties to provide work & means of livelihood for citizens. The activities of the individual must not clash with the interest of the whole but must be pursued within the framework of Nat. activity & must be for the general good. Demand therefore abolition of incomes unearned by work & emancipation from interest charges. Confiscation of all war profits. Nationalization of all business trusts. Great industries shall be organization on a profit sharing basis. The extensive development of provision for old age. & ed. facilities for specially gifted children of poor parents at the expense of the state. Our Nat. can only achieve permanent well being from within on the principles of common interest before self interest.

⇥ Mussolini

We were the first to assert that the more complicated the forms assumed by civilization the more restricted the freedom of the individual must become.

⇥ Letter From a Young American Socialist to Friend Around 1968

It is my life, my business, my religion, my hobby, my bread & meat. I have already been in jail because of my ideas & if necessary I am ready to go before a firing squad. We have a cause to fight for—a def. purpose in life. We have a morale an esprit de corps such as no capitalist army ever had—a devotion to our cause that no religious order can touch.

⧫ Anonymous

When govt. doesn't know what it's supposed to do, it ends up trying to do everything.

⚜

Freedom rests and always will on individual responsibility, individ. integrity, individ. effort, individ. courage, & individual religious faith.

⚜

We must pay a price for freedom but whatever the price it's only half the cost of doing without it.

⇥ **John F. Kennedy**

The scarlet thread running through the thoughts & actions of people all over the world is the delegation of great problems to the all-absorbing leviathan—the state . . . Every time that we try to lift a problem to the govt., to the same extent we are sacrificing the liberties of the people.

⇥ **John Cotton, 18th Century**

Let all the world learn to give mortal man no greater power than they are content they shall use—for use it they will.

⇥ Lord Denning on Economy

What matters is that each man should be free to develop his own personality to the full; and the only duties which restrict this freedom are those which are necessary to enable everyone to do the same. Whenever these interests are nicely balanced the scale goes down on the side of freedom.

⇥ Lord Acton 70 Years After Adoption of U.S. Constitution

They had solved with astonishing ease & unexampled success 2 probs. which had heretofore baffled the capacity of the most enlightened nations. They had contrived a system of Fed. govt. which prodigiously increased nat. power & yet respected local liberties & authorities & they had founded it on the prin. of equality without surrendering the securities of property & freedom.

⇥ Sen. Benjamin H. Hill, 1867

I do not dread those corps. as instruments of power to destroy this country, because there are 1000 agencies which can regulate, restrain and control them; but there is a corp. we may all dread. That corp. is the Fed. govt. From the aggression of this corp. there can be no safety, if it is allowed to go beyond the bounds, the well defined limits of its power. I dread nothing so much as the exercise of ungranted & doubtful power by this govt. It is in my opinion, the danger of dangers to the future of this country. Let us be sure we keep it always within its limits. If this great, ambitious, ever growing corp. becomes oppressive, who shall check it? If it becomes wayward, who shall control it? If it becomes unjust, who shall trust it? As sentinels of the country's watchtower, Senators, I beseech you to watch & guard with sleepless dread that corp. which can make all property & hope its playthings in an hour & its victims forever. Regulations once imposed, are never withdrawn but usually made tighter & tighter.

☙ Herbert Aptheker, "Daily World," Communist Paper

This capitalism—this system born of the slave trade & centuries of slavery, of child labor & the abuse of women, of contempt for those who labor & produce, with its adornments of male supremacy & elitism & racism and its products of colonialism & robber wars— this capitalism, through its politicians & its pen men, dares to lecture the world of socialism about morality & human rights. This system with its ghettos & barriers, its colonies & unemployment its impoverishments & hunger, its slums & closed libraries, its massage par- lors & closed hospitals—this putrid system literally stinking up the atmosphere gives lessons in ethics to Communists!

✒ S.D.S. Leader During Campus Riots in the 1960s

It's not reform we're after. It's the destruction of your stinking rotten society & you'd better learn that fast.

✒ James Madison, The Federalist Papers

The 1st question that offers itself is whether the general form & aspect of the govt. be strictly republican. It is evident that no other form would be reconcilable with the genius of the people of Am.; with the fundamental principles of the revolution or with that honorable determination which animates every notary of freedom to rest all our pol. experiments on the capacity of mankind for self govt.

❧ Thomas Jefferson, 1st 18 Words Only Are Engraved On Memorial

Nothing is more certainly written in the book of fate, than that these people are to be free; nor is it less certain, that the two races, equally free, cannot live in the same govt. Nature, habit, opinion have drawn indelible lines of distinction between them. It is still in our power to direct the process of emancipation and deportation, peaceably, and in such slow degree, as that the evil will wear off insensibly, and their place be, pari passu, filled up by free white "laborers."

❧ Aesop

Bad as any govt. may be it is seldom worse than anarchy.

⊰⊱ Thomas Paine

Govt. is a necessary evil—let us have as little of it as possible.

⊰⊱ Justice O. W. Holmes

Strike for the jugular. Reduce taxes *and spending*. Keep govt. poor and remain free.

⊰⊱ "Take sides"—Phil. Romulo

Freedom is precious—defend it—it is not cheap, nor easy, nor neutral. It is dear & hard & real—take sides for frdm. or you will lose it.

⊰⋈ Abraham Lincoln

The people are the rightful masters of both Congresses and courts, not to overthrow the Const. but to overthrow the men who pervert the Const.

⊰⋈ Herbert Hoover

The key is that among us there is greater frdm. for the individ. man & woman than in any other great nat. In the Const. & in the Bill of Rts. are enumerated the specific frdms. Then there are a doz. other frdms. which are not a matter of specific law—such as frdm. to choose our own callings, frdm. to quit a job & seek another, frdm. to buy or not to buy, frdm. for each man to venture & to protect his success, *always* subject to the rise of his neighbors. In short we have frdm. of choice.

✒ Thomas Wolfe

To every man his chance, to very man regardless of his birth, his shining golden opportunity. To every man the rt. to live, to work, to be himself & to become whatever his manhood & his vision can combine to make him. This is the promise of America.—Rise & Fall

✒ Legend Declaration of Independence

They may turn every tree into a gallows, every home into a grave & yet the words of that parchment can never die . . . To the mechanic in the workshop they will speak hope; to the slaves in the mines freedom . . . Sign that parchment. Sign if the next moment the noose is around your neck—for that parchment will be the textbook of freedom—the Bible of the rights of man forever.

⇥ Samuel Gompers Described Govt.
Social Insurance

Menace to the rights, the welfare & the lib. of the working man—cannot remove or prevent poverty—can't take risk out—without denying freedom of choice.

ON WAR

⇥ Rev. Muhlenberg

On a bright Sunday morning at the outbreak of the Rev. War—the Rev. was preaching his sermon when he was handed a note.—paused read the note then silently removed his ministerial robe. He was wearing the uniform of Wash's army. "My friends there is a time to preach and a time to fight. This is a time to fight."

⇥ John Stuart Mill

War is an ugly thing. But not the ugliest of things. The decayed & degraded st. of moral & patriotic feeling which things nothing is worth a war is worse. A man who has nothing he cares about more than his personal safety is a miserable creature & has no chance of being free unless made & kept so by the exertions of better men than himself.

⇥ Anonymous

I want to say something about Army. When all the slick pants politicians have finished their work, and all the speeches are finished in the Senate & the House, and all the ultimatums have been issued and rejected, there comes a time when a soldier with a gun stands to defend his country. And so in the final analysis the most important thing we have are the fighting men in this country, because it will be them & no one else who will see that our freedoms are perpetuated for our children & for their children.

⤳

Of all the men who have died in battle to preserve what we have today 88% wore the uniform of the U.S. Army.

⤨ Dean of Canterbury, Talking About Civil War, 1863 (Rev. Henry Alford)

Denounced the U.S. for: "Its reckless and fruitless maintenance of the most cruel and unprincipled war in the history of the world." (The war that ended slavery)

❧ Thomas Jefferson

If we are forced into a war, we must give up differences of opinion and united as one nation to defend our country.

❧ George Washington

Dinner dialogue at Mt. Vernon between Lafayette and GW:

L: "George you Americans even in war & desperate times have a superb spirit. You are happy & you are confident. Why is it?

GW: "There is freedom, there is space for a man to be alone & think & there are friends who owe each other nothing but affection."

⇥ Sun Tzu 2500 Years Ago

An army is only the instrument which administers the coup de grace to an enemy already defeated by intel. ops which separated the enemy from his allies, corrupted his officials, spread misleading info. & correctly assessed his strengths & weaknesses—winning 100 battles is not the acme of skill—to subdue the enemy without fighting is the acme of skill.

⇥ Winston Churchill

Still if you will not fight for the right when you can win without bloodshed; if you will not fight when your victory will be sure & not too costly; you may come to the moment when you'll have to fight with all the odds against you & only a precarious chance of survival. There may even be a worse case. You may have to fight when there is *no* chance of victory because it is better to perish than to live as slaves.

✎ J.F.K.

There can be only one possible defense policy for the U.S. It can be expressed in one word—the word is 1st. I do not mean 1st when—I don't mean 1st if—I mean 1st, period.

✎ Dwight Eisenhower

The vital element in keeping the peace is our military establishment. Our arms must be mighty, ready for instant action, so that no potential aggressor may be tempted to risk its own destruction.

⇥ Demosthenes, 1000 Years Ago— Athenian Mkt. Place

What sane man would let another man's words rather than his deeds tell him who is at war & who is at peace with him.

⇥ General G. Macarthur, West Point '62

I do not know the dignity of their birth but I do know the glory of their death. They died unquestioning, uncomplaining, with faith in their hearts, and on their lips the hope that we would go on to victory.

❧ Prayer Of Aristophanes Among Ruins of Greek Temple Destroyed in the Peloponnesian War

From the murmur & subtlety of suspicion with which we vex one, another give us rest. Make a new beginning mingle again among the kindred of the nations with the alchemy of love; and with some finer essence of forbearance, temper our minds.

❧ Vladimir Lenin

Great historical questions can be solved only by violence, & organization of violence in the modern struggle is a military organization.

❦

It would be madness to renounce coercion.

⇥ Nikita Khrushchev

We must realize that we cannot exist eternally, for a long time . . . one of us must go to his grave. The Ams. & the west do not want to go to their grave either so what can be done? We must push them to their grave.

⇥ Feb. 1961, Gus Hall, American Communist Party, Funeral E. Dennis

I dream of the hour when the last Congressman is strangled to death on the guts of the last preacher—and since the Christians seem to love to sing about blood, why not give them a little of it? Slit the throats of their children & draw them over the mourners bench and the pulpit, & allow them to drown in their own blood, & then see whether they enjoy singing those hymns.

❧ Winston Churchill, The Gathering Storm

It is my purpose . . . to show how easily the tragedy of the Second World War could have been prevented; how the malice of the wicked was reinforced by the weakness of the virtuous; how the structure and habits of democratic states, unless they are welded into larger organisms, lack those elements of persistence and conviction which can alone give security to humble masses; how, even in matters of self-preservation, no policy is pursued for even ten or fifteen years at a time. We shall see how the counsels of prudence and restraint may become the prime agents of mortal danger; how the middle course adopted from desires for safety and a quiet life may be found to lead direct to the bull's-eye of disaster.

ON THE
PEOPLE

⚜

The Am. people have a genius for great & unselfish deeds—into the hands of Am. God has placed an afflicted mankind. For men who could not see that what they firmly believed was liberalism added up to socialism could scarcely be expected to see what added up to communism. Any charge of comm. enraged them precisely because they could not grasp the differences between themselves and those against whom it was made.

⇥ Hilaire Belloc

We sit by & watch the Barbarian, we tolerate him; in the long stretches of peace we are not afraid. We are tickled by his irreverence, his comic invasion of our old certitudes and our fixed creeds refreshes us; we laugh. But as we laugh we are watched by large & awful faces from beyond; and on these faces there is no smile.

⇥ Daniel Webster

I sought for the greatness of Am. in her commodious harbors & her ample rivers & it was not there. In her fertile fields & boundless prairies & it was not there. In her rich mines & her vast world commerce & it was not there. Not until I went to the churches of Am. & heard her pulpits aflame with righteousness did I understand the secret of her genius and her power. Am. is great because she is good & if Am. ever ceases to be good Am. will cease to be great.

⇥ Goethe Letter to Eckerman, 1828

The truth must be repeated again & again because error is constantly being preached round about us. And not only by isolated individuals but by the majority. In the newspapers & encyclopedias, in the schools and Universities everywhere error is dominant, securely & comfortable ensconced in pub. opinion which is on its side.

⊰⊱ **Chinese Proverb, 400 B.C.**

When the music of a nation becomes fast, wild & discordant it shows the nation is in confusion.

⊰⊱ **Abba Eban**

History shows that men & nations behave reasonably only when they have exhausted all other alternatives.

⊰⊱ **Alexander Hamilton**

It will be of little avail to the people that laws are made by men of their own choice if the laws be so voluminous that they cannot be read, or so incoherent that they cannot be understood: if they be repealed or revised before the are promulgated, or undergo such incessant changes that no man who knows what the law is today can guess what it will be tomorrow.

⇥ **Thomas Jefferson, 1810**

A strict observance of the written law is doubtless one of the highest duties of a good citizen but it is not the highest. The law of necessity, of self preservation, of saving our country by a scrupulous adherence to the written law, would be to lose the law itself, with life, liberty, property & all those who are enjoying them with us; thus absurdly sacrificing the end to the means.

⚜

The lottery is a wonderful thing; it lays the taxation only on the willing.

⁓❦⁓

To compel a man to furnish contributions of money for the propagation of opinions which he disbelieves is sinful and tyrannical.

⁓❦⁓

If we can prevent govt. from wasting the labor of the people under the pretense of taking care of them—they must become happy.

⁓❦⁓

The boys of the rising generation are to be the men of the next & the sole guardian of the principles we deliver over to them.

⌘

It is in the natural course of events that liberty recedes & govt. grows.

⌘

I never considered a dif. of opinion in pols. in religion, in phil. as cause for withdrawing from a friend.

⌘

The bulk of mankind are school boys through life. Ed. is the true corrective of abuses of const. power.

⌘

The force of public opinion cannot be resisted when permitted freely to be expressed. Whenever the people are well informed, they can be trusted with their own govt.

⇥ **George Washington**

It is not consistent with reason or justice to expect that one set of men should make a sacrifice of property, domestic ease & happiness encounter the rigid of the field, the perils & vicissitudes of war to obtain these blessings which every citizen will enjoy on common with them without some compensation.

⋅⋆⋅

If any body of people are allowed to go unpunished to rise & disobey any law, all law & order would soon vanish.

⚜

We must never parley or haggle with sedition, treason or lawlessness but must strike a blow that cannot be parried & at once.

⚜

Freedom from want must never be interpreted as freedom from the necessity to struggle.

⚜

To Lafayette 1791: The tumultuous populace of the large cities are ever to be dreaded. Their indiscriminate violence frustrated for all time all pub. authority & its consequences are sometimes extensive & terrible.

❧ Alan C. Brownfield

Ed. which trains in skills but does not teach values is deficient. Its emphasis today all too often does not seek to make the individual a thinking person but seeks to condition him to the generally accepted view of the common good.

❧ C. S. Lewis

The older ed. was a kind of propagation—men transmitted manhood to man—the new is merely propaganda.

❧ Ortega Y. Gasset

Civilization is not self supporting—it is artificial and requires the artist or the artisan. If you want to make

use of the advantages of civilization but are not prepared to concern yourself with the upholding of civilization—you are done.

⇥ **Edmund Burke**

It is a general popular error to imagine the loudest
complainers for the pub. to be the most anxious for
its welfare.

⇥ **Abe Lincoln**

Labor was prior to capitalism but property is the fruit
of labor. Prop. is desirable & is a positive good to the
world. That some should be rich shows that others may
become rich & hence is just encouragement to industry
& enterprise.

⚜

A man may be loyal to his govt. & still be opposed to the peculiar prins. & practices of the admin. in power.

⚜

With public sentiment behind you, anything is possible. Without it, nothing is possible. Therefore, he who influences public sentiment performs a vastly more significant act than he who simply meets statutes.

⧏ Winston Churchill

The destiny of man is not measured by material computations. When great forces are on the move in the world we learn we are spirits not animals. There is something going on in time & space & beyond time & space which whether we like it or not spells duty.

⇥ F.D.R. on Public Employee Strikes

I want to emphasize my conviction that militant tactics have no place in the functions of any organizations of govt. employees. A strike of pub. emps. manifests nothing less than an intent on their part to prevent or obstruct the operations of govt. until their demands are satisfied. Such action looking toward the paralysis of govt. by those who have sworn to support it is unthinkable & intolerable.

⇥ J.F.K.

We are in danger of losing something solid at the core. We are losing that pilgrim & pioneer spirit of initiative and independence—that old-fashioned Spartan devotion to duty, honor & country.

Ibn Khaldoun (Moslem Phil. 14th Century)

At the beginning of the dynasty taxation yields a large revenue from small assessments. At the end of the Dynasty taxation yields a small revenue from large assessments.

Cicero

A nation can survive its fools & even the ambitious but it cannot survive treason from within. For the traitor appears no traitor; he speaks in an accent familiar to his victims & wears their face & their garments . . . he rots the soul of the nation. He works secretly & unknown in the night to undermine the pillars of the city; he infects the body politic so that it can no longer resist. A murderer is less to be feared.

᭱

Had there not been older men to undo the damage done by the young, there would be no states.

᭱ Aspasia, Friend of Socrates, 429 B.C.

I am baffled by Sparta, by its ugliness, its bigotry, its single minded dedication to turning out citizens who are anonymous efficient instruments of war. They are hemmed in by prejudice, allowed no contact with the outside world, have no choice but to believe what they are told.

᭱ William Penn

If men be good govt. cannot then be bad.

✥ Arnold Toynbee

Hist. is the pattern of silken slippers descending the stairs & the thunder of hobnail boots coming up.

✥ Bastiat Addressing National Assembly—France, 12/12/1849

When the people are encouraged to turn to govt. to settle all of their problems for them the basis of revolutions is thereby established. For then the people expect the govt. to provide them with all the material things they want. And when these things are not forthcoming they resort to violence to get them & why not since the govt. itself has told them that these responsibilities belong to govt. rather than to them? I am convinced that the revolution would not be possible, if the only relationship between govt. & the people was to guaranty them their liberty & security.

⤔ **Bastiat**

People are beginning to realize that the apparatus of govt. is costly. But what they do not know is that the burden falls inevitably on them.

⤔ **Founder Salvation Army—William Booth, At 83 & Nearly Blind**

While women weep as they do now—I'll fight. While little children go hungry as they do now—I'll fight. While there is a poor lost girl upon the street—I'll fight. While there yet remains one dark soul without the light of God I'll fight. I'll fight to the very end.

❧ Dr. James Conant

The greater proportion of our youth who attend private schools the greater the threat to our Dem. Unity.

❧ National Ed. Association 1934 Report

A dying laissez-faire must be completely destroyed and all of us including the owners must be subjected to a large degree of social control.

❧ Yrs. Ago John D. Rockefeller Put His Asst. Fred Gates in Charge of His Tax Free Ed. Board. Paper No. 1 Said:

In our dreams we have limitless resources & the people yield themselves with perfect docility to our molding hands. The present educational conventions fade from our minds & unhampered by tradition we work our own good will upon a grateful & responsive rural folk.

⊰ৰ Samuel Gompers

Doing for people what they can & ought to do for themselves is a dangerous experiment. In the last analysis the welfare of the workers depends on their own initiative. Whatever is done under the guise of philanthropy for *social morality* which in any way lessens initiative is the greatest crime that can be committed against the toilers. Let social busy bodies & professional morals experts in their pads reflect upon the perils they rashly invite under the pretense of social welfare.

⤟

The company that doesn't make a profit is the enemy of the working man.

⇥ U.S. National Labor Paper

The time has come to put into effect a single integrated Fed. system guaranteeing cradle to grave security against the hazards of illness, disability, work injury & old age.

⇥ Adolph Hitler

We shall banish want, we shall banish fear. The essence of National Socialism is human welfare rooted in a fuller life for every German from childhood to old age.

⊰≫ Dr. Alex Fraser Tytler on Athens Fall 2000 Years Ago

A democracy cannot exist as a permanent form of govt. It can only exist until the voters discover they can vote themselves largess out of the pub. treasury. From that moment on the majority always votes for the candidate promising the most benefits from the public treasury with the result the democracy always collapses over a loose fiscal policy always to be followed by a dictatorship.

⊰≫ Leonard Read

Regardless of theoretical pretentions, socialism is nothing but the application of dictatorial power.

⇥ **Anonymous**

In the late 60's, a group of drs. formed an org. to ed. people about Socialized medicine. The I.R.S. ruled— "opposing socialism in the med. or other segments of the economoy or supporting the principles of individual lib. & freedom of the individual in the med. profession or elsewhere are not in our opinion per se educational functions or objectives & you are not entitled to take deductions from your Fed. income tax."

⇥ **Poem**

The snow was blowing out of doors—the drifts were piling high, and I could see the pedestrians as they were passing by. The faces of my Irish friends came dimly through the glass, as they trudged the icy streets to worship at their mass. I watched a while, went back to bed and cuddled safe & sound as they braved those icy blasts on a sacred duty bound. I envy them their strength of heart, the faith that they renew, but on an ice cold Sunday morn it's good to be a Jew.

ᐳᛱ Poem "Teacher"—Clark Mollenhoff

You are the molders of their dreams—the Gods who build or crush their young beliefs of Rt. or Wrong. You are the spark that sets aflame the poet's hand or lights the flame of some great singer's song. You are the God of the young—the very young. You are the guardians of a million dreams. Your every smile or frown can heal or pierce a heart. Yours are 100 lives—1000 lives. Yours the pride of loving them, the sorrow too. Your patient work, your touch make you the God of hope—that fills their souls with dreams—to make those dreams come true.

⊰⊱ Lord Moulton

True civilization is measured by the extent of obedience to the unenforceable.

⊰⊱ 2nd Thessalonians 3:10

If anyone does not want to work then he should not eat either.

⊰⊱ Acts 19:32

Some therefore cried one thing & some another for the assembly was confused; & the more part knew not wherefore they were come together.

⇥ **Bible Judges 9—Parable**

The Trees went forth to anoint a King over themselves. The olive tree, the fig tree, the vine—all declined to abandon their productive pursuits to become a King. So the trees then turned to the bramble and the bramble accepted.

⇥ **Dr. Goebbels**

Whoever can conquer the street will conquer the state one day for every form of power politics & any dictatorially run state has its roots in the street. We cannot have enough of public demonstrations for that is far & away the most emphatic way of demonstrating ones will to govern. It means a sight more than elec. statistics. When we can see our men thousands of them marching up & down the streets that is nothing short of mobilization for power.

❧ Judge Learned Hand

There is nothing sinister in so arranging ones affairs as to keep taxes just as low as possible. Nobody owes any public duty to pay more than the law demands. Taxes are enforced exactions not vol. contributions. To demand more in the name of morals is mere cant.

❧

Anyone may so arrange his affairs that his taxes shall be as low as possible, he is not bound to choose that pattern which will best pay the treasury; there is not even a patriotic duty to *increase* one's taxes.

❧ J. Edgar Hoover

The cure for crime is not the electric chair but the high chair.

✥ Paul McCracken

It is interesting to speculate what would happen if a delegation from the Economic Dept. of U. of Outer Space were asked to fly around this planet & see if they could sort out the planned & unplanned economies. They would in fact probably get them sorted out; but they might as well have the labels on the 2 lists reversed. Of course the so-called unplanned economies aren't unplanned at all. They rely on an extremely sophisticated system of planning reflected in the mechanisms of institutions of the market to organize ec. activity & to generate material progress.

✥ Prof. Geo. Sternlieb

The billions of $ that are being spent on the urban poor by all levels of govt. go mainly to support a growing W.F. bureaucracy of teacher-aides, youth workers, clerks, supervisors, key punchers, & people's lawyers.

The bureauc. is sustained by the plight of the poor, the threat of the poor, the misery of the poor, but it yields little in the way of loaves & fishes to the poor.

⇥ John Ramsay McCulloch, Scotch Ec., More—100 Years Ago

The moment you abandon the cardinal principle of extracting from all individuals the same proportion of their income or their property you are at sea without rudder or compass & there is no amount of injustice or folly you may not commit.

⇥ A Florida Bus Attendant—Ralph Bradford

Human society is built & can only be built upon a foundation of citizenship accountability. The strength of a nation is not its legal machinery, but the moral stamina & courage of its people. The law is but the codification of their conscience. There are not enough laws & never will be, to keep a society stable if its members no longer will it. There are not enough policemen, courts, judges or prisons, nor ever can be to prevent the death of a civilization whose people no longer care. Law enforcement is for the criminal few; it collapses if it must be enforced against the many. When the sense of personal accountability is no longer present in majority strength, then no legal device known to man can hold the society together. *Freedom is a timely torch blazing in the dark.*

⇥ **Herbert Spencer, Essay, Self-Defense and Paternalism**

Of the pauper—the more you assist him the more he wants. Of the busy man the more he has to do the more he can do. A whole nation must be so—that just in proportion as its members are little helped by extraneous power they will become self helping and in proportion as they are much helped they will become helpless.

⇥ Hiram Johnson, 1910, Los Angeles

In our city we have drunk the dregs of the cup of infamy; we have been betrayed by pub. officials & sold out by those we trusted. But in our city we have never had anyone so vicious, so venomous, so putrescent or so vile as Harrison Gray Otis of the L.A. Times. The one blot on the escutcheon of L.A.—the bar sinister upon your city is Harrison Gray Otis of the L.A. Times. There he sits in senile dementia, with gangrene heart & rotting brain, grimacing at our every attempt at reform & chattering away in impotent rage while he goes down to his foul grave in snarling infamy.

⤞ Will Rogers

You are sentenced to prison as long as it's made comfortable for you & your desire to remain. In checking out let the warden know, so he will know how many there will be for supper.

⤠

Even when you make out a tax return on the level you don't know if you are a crook or a martyr.

⤠

Every time a lawyer writes something, he is not writing for posterity. He's writing so endless others of his craft can make a living out of trying to figure out what he said. Course perhaps he hadn't really said anything, that's what makes it hard to explain.

⚜

The minute you read something & you can't understand it, you can be sure it was written by a lawyer. Then if you give it to another lawyer to read & he don't know just what it means then you can be sure it was drawn up by a lawyer. If it's in a few words and its plain & understandable only one way it was written by a non-lawyer.

⤙ Norman Thomas

Socialism is a scare word to many but it has a high degree of acceptance by people who hotly deny it. Nov. 21 1957, N.Y. Times (could be '54).

⇥ Thomas Jefferson

I place economy among the 1st & most important virtues, & public debt as the greatest of dangers to be feared. To preserve our independence we must not let our rulers load us with perpetual debt. If we run into such debt we must be taxed in our meat & drink, in our necessities & in our comforts, in our labor & amusements. If we can prevent the govt. from wasting the labor of the people *under the pretense of caring for them*, they will be happy.

⇤ Samuel Gompers

Only resentment is aroused & the end is not gained. Only thru moral suasion & appeal to men's reason can a movement succeed.

❧ Lord Macaulay to Hon. H. S. Randall—N.Y. (Grandson, Thom. Jeff.), May 23 1857

As I said before, when society has entered on this downward progress either civilization or lib. must perish. Either some Caesar or Napoleon will seize the reins of govt. with a strong hand, or your rep. will be fearfully plundered & laid waste by barbarians in the 20th century as the Roman emp. was in the 5th; with this diff., that the Huns & vandals who ravaged the Roman Emp. came from without & that your Huns & vandals will be engendered form within your country by your own institutions.

⇥ Poem

His horse went dead & his mule went lame,
And he lost 6 cows in the poker game.
Then a hurricane came on a summer's day
And blew the house where he lived away
An earthquake came when that was gone
And swallowed the land the house stood on
And then the tax collector came around
& charged him up with the hole in the ground.

ON RELIGION

❧ Whittaker Chambers

My eye came to rest on the delicate convolutions of her ear. Those intricate perfect ears the thought passed through my mind—no those ears were not (as the comms. say) created by any chance coming together of atoms in nature. I didn't know it at the time but God had laid his finger on my forehead.

⊰❊ Thomas Jefferson

The God who gave us life gave us liberty—can the liberties of a nation be secure when we have removed a conviction that these liberties are the gift of God?

⊰❊ George Washington

Despair my fellow countrymen of ever teaching citizenship save on the basis of immorality & abandon all hope of teaching morality on any other foundation than religion for the nation that forgot God has never been allowed to endure.

⇥ Patrick Henry

Perfect freedom is necessary to the health & vigor of both commerce & citizenship & both will have freedom concurrently or neither will have it at all.

❧

We have it within our power to begin the world over again.

❧

Those who expect to reap the blessing of freedom must undertake to support it.

❧

I have no light to illuminate the pathway of the future save that which falls over my shoulder from the past.

⊰꓿   John Dickinson, Signer, Declaration of Independence

It is not our duty to leave wealth to our children, but it is our duty to leave liberty to them. We have counted the cost of this content & we find nothing so dreadful as voluntary slavery.

⊰꓿   Abe Lincoln

I should be the most presumptuous blockhead upon this footstool if I for one day thought that I could discharge the duties which have come upon me, since

I came to this place, without the aid & enlightenment of one who is stronger & wiser than all others.

❧ Antigone to the Legislature: Sophocles

You who are mortal cannot change the infallible, unwritten laws of heaven They did not begin today or yesterday, but they are everlasting & none can tell the hour that saw their birth. I would not from fear of any human edict, incur the God-inflicted penalty of disobeying divine law.

❧ William Penn

If men will not be governed by God (that is to be honest, truthful, diligent, fair & just to all) then they must be governed by tyrants.

ᛞ Numbers 6:24–26

The Lord bless thee & keep thee. The Lord make his face to shine upon thee & be gracious unto thee. The Lord lift up his countenance upon thee & give thee peace.

ᛞ Commandments

Thou shalt love the Lord thy God with all thy heart & with all thy soul & with all thy mind—this is the 1st & great commandment. (& the 2nd is like unto it).

⚜

Thou shalt love thy neighbor as thyself. On these 2 commandments, hang all the law & the prophets.

⋙ **Irish Blessing**

May the road rise to meet you. May the wind be always at your back. May the sun shine warm upon your face, the rain fall soft upon your fields & until we meet again, may God hold you in the hollow of his hand.

⋙ **The Rangers Prayer**

Oh God whose end is justice, Whose strength is all our stay, Be near & bless my mission as I go forth today. Let wisdom guide my actions, let courage fill my heart and help me, Lord, in every hour to do a Ranger's part, Protect when danger threatens, sustain when trails are rough; help me to keep my standard high and smile at each rebuff. When might comes down upon me, I pray thee, Lord, be nigh, whether lonely scout, or camped, under the Texas sky. Keep me, oh God, in life and when my days shall end, forgive my sins and take me in, For Jesus' sake, Amen.

⇥ High Flight—John Gillespie Magee, Jr.

Oh! I have slipped the surly bonds of Earth
And danced the skies on laughter-silvered wings;
Sunward I've climbed, and joined the tumbling
   mirth
Of sun-split clouds—and done a hundred things
You have not dreamed of—wheeled and soared
   and swung
High in the sunlit silence. Hov'ring there,
I've chased the shouting wind along, and flung
My eager craft through footless halls of airs. . . .
Up, up the long, delirious, burning blue
I've topped the wind-swept heights with easy grace,
Where never lark, or even eagle, flew;
And, while with silent, lifting mind I've trod
The high untrespassed sanctity of space,
Put out my hand, and touched the face of God.

(Written by a 19-year-old American volunteer with the Royal Canadian Air Force, who was killed in training December 11, 1941)

⇥ **Anonymous**

*You cannot pray the Lord's prayer & even once
   say 'I,'*
*You cannot pray the Lord's prayer & even once
   say 'my'*
*You cannot pray the Lord's prayer & not include
   another;*
*You cannot ask for daily bread & not include
   your brother.*
For others are included in each & every plea;
From the very beginning it never once says me.

[Unknown, Christian Reader, Vol. 32, No. 3]

⇥ **Isaiah 1:18**

Come let us reason together.

⇥ Isaiah 19:20

If ye be willing ye shall eat the good of the land—but if ye refuse & rebel—ye shall be devoured with the sword. For the mouth of the Lord hath spoken it.

Thomas Jefferson Prior to Writing Dec. of Independence, Inscribed on Jefferson Memorial, Wash. D.C.

The God who gave us life gave us lib. Can the libs. of a nat. be secure when we have removed a conviction that these libs. are the gift of God?

⤴ 1962—St. N.Y. Proposed Prayer for Its Schools

Almighty God we acknowledge our dependence on thee and we beg thy blessing upon us, our parents, our teachers & our country.—U.S. Supreme Ct. Ruled it Unconst.

THE WORLD

⤛

⤛ **Sen. Fulbright**

It is possible that if Mao Tse Tung & Ho Chi Minh had not borne the title of Communist but otherwise had done exactly what they have done in their 2 countries, we would have accepted their victories over their domestic rivals & lived with them in peace.

⇥ **Thomas Jefferson**

Letter to John Jay Urging a Strong Navy & Prompt Retailiation Against Any Aggressor Seizing or Harassing U.S. Shipping:

⚘

Speedy retaliation was necessary because an insult unanswered is the parent of many others."

⇥ **RR's Wisdom**

The path of history is littered with the bones of dead empires. If we are to follow we will have no decades or centuries for leisurely decay & disintegration. The enemy at our gates is combat lean & hard. Hungry for all we've created.

⇥ Winston Churchill

On the Day After Munich 1938—All is over. Silent, mournful, abandoned, broken Czechoslovakia recedes into the darkness. And do not suppose that this is the end. This is only the beginning of the reckoning. This is only the 1st sip, the 1st foretaste of a bitter cup which will be proffered to us year by year, unless by a supreme recovery of moral health and martial vigor we ride again and take our stand for freedom as in the olden time.

⇥ Cicero

We are taxed in our bread & wine—in our income & our investments—on our land & property—not only for base creatures who do not deserve the name of men—for foreign nations who bow to us & accept our largesse—& promise to assist in keeping the power—these mendicant nations who will destroy us when we show a moment of weakness—or when the treasury is bare—& surely it is becoming bare—were they bound to us by ties of love they would not ask for our gold—they hate & despise us—& who shall say we are worthy of more.

✎ Book Uncommon Sense by James McGregor Burns

The way in which Ams. live, the quality of Am. life is the most important aspect of Am. foreign policy today. The Democratic & above all the open way in which we have faced our social & economic problems has been the most impressive & influential aspect of Am. foreign policy not only in dealing with the Soviet U. but in our relations with other peoples in the world. This has little to do with Am. security—it has much to do with the moral worth of the Am. Svc. & the standards it could set for the world . . . The Am. declaration of independence is cited & copied throughout the emerging countries. Its precepts have proved contagious. At the very least Am. world leadership should so act as not to dishonor the ideas it has given to the world; at the most, it should act so as to help make them a reality. But paradoxically this cannot be forced upon others; each people must make its own independence, achieve its own liberty & equality.

⇥ Israeli Scientist

Those nat's. which have put liberty ahead of equality have ended up doing better by equality than those with the reverse principles.

⇥ Vladimir Lenin

As long as capitalism & socialism exist we cannot live in peace. Socialists without ceasing to be socialists cannot oppose any kind of war.

⛬

To tie one's hands in advance & to openly tell an enemy who is presently armed that we *will* fight him & when is stupidity.

⚞ Andrei Gromyko "Foreign Policy— Soviet Union" 1975

The communist party subordinates all its theoretical & practical activity in the sphere of international relations to the task of strengthening the positions of socialism & in the interests of further developing & deepening the world revolutionary process.

⇥ Pravda

The world wide nature of our communist program is not mere talk *but* all embracing & all blood soaked reality.

⇥ Text Book

If we could effectively kill the Nat. pride & patriotism of just one generation we will have won that country. Therefore there must be continued propaganda abroad to undermine the loyalty of the citizen in general & the teenagers in particular.

⇥ Dmitriy Manuilsky Lenin School for Pol. Warfare—1930s

War to the hilt between communism & capitalism is inevitable. But today we are too weak to strike. Our day will come in 30 or 40 years. First we must lull the capitalist nations to sleep with the greatest overtures of peace & disarmament known in history, and when their guard is dropped, we shall smash them with our clenched fist.

⇥ Russian Diplomat

We'll be over to finish the takeover sooner than you think. You know that a mixed economy is not permanent & you have already mixed so much socialism with your formerly free ec. that you cannot take it back or change. You are coming all the way into full socialism. We don't have to fight you or urge you. We shall simply wait until you walk voluntarily into our camp.

⇥ Alex Solzhenitsyn

At one time there was no comparison between the strength of the U.S.S.R. and yours. Then it became equal to yours. Soon it will be 2 to 1 then 3 & finally it will be 5–1 and it is fully determined to destroy your society.

⇤ Former Senator William Benton

We must abolish the '48 Balkanized units each in turn into scores of hundreds of local dist. so as to compete with Soviet Russia.

ON
CHARACTER

⇥ Ralph Waldo Emerson

The hero is no braver than an ordinary man—but he is brave 5 min. longer.

❧ Anonymous Quotes

The greatest liar has his believers. If a lie be believed for only an hour it has done its work. Falsehood flies & truth comes limping after; so that when men come to be undeceived it is too late; the tale has had its effect.

Greatness is measured by your kindness, your ed. & intellect. By your modesty. Your ignorance is betrayed by your suspicions & prejudices—your real caliber is measured by the consideration and thoughtfulness you have for others.

A gentle[man] always says & does the kindest thing.

⌘

Liberty is always dangerous but it's the safest thing to have.

⌘

Man's capacity for justice makes democracy possible but man's inclination to injustice makes democracy necessary.

⌘

Reality may be a rough road but escape from it is a precipice.

RONALD REAGAN

❧

To sin by silence when they should protest makes cowards of men.

❧

Even moderation should not be practiced to excess.

❧

He who would have nothing to do with thorns should never attempt to gather flowers.

❧

People are lonely who build walls instead of bridges.

᳙

Just think how happy you'd be if you lost everything you have right now & then got it back.

᳙   Swiss Author Henri Frederic Amiel

Truth is violated by falsehood but it is outraged by silence.

᳙   Henry Marshall

Out of the ghetto comes an Al Smith, Eddie Cantor, Sam Levinson, Joe Louis, Babe Ruth & a mil. others. They just couldn't understand that they didn't have a chance. They just couldn't be stopped from using disadvantages as advantages. They knew intuitively what Confucius had said, 'that defeat was not getting knocked down—but in not getting up.'

⇥ Robert Browning

Grow old with me—the best is yet to be—the last of life for which the first was made.

⇥ Chinese Proverb

The beginning of wisdom is calling things by their right name.

⇥ Goethe

If everybody swept his own doorstep the whole world would be clean.

⇥ Mao

It is better for a woman to marry a man who loves her than to marry a man she loves.

⇥ Thomas Jefferson

HARMONY in the married state is the very 1st object to be aimed at. Happiness by the domestic fireside is the 1st boon of heaven.

❧

State a moral case to a plowman and a Professor. The farmer will decide it as well & often better because he has not been led astray by any artificial rules.

Letter to Grandson Warning Against Disputes with Students:

Keep aloof from them as you would from an infected subject of yellow fever or pestilence. Consider yourself when with them as among the patients of bedlam needing medical care more than normal counsel. Be a listener only, keeping within yourself the habit of silence especially on politics No good can ever result from any attempts to set one of these fiery zealots to rights either on fact or principle. They are determined as to the facts they will believe & the opinions on which they will act. Get by them as you would by an angry bull. It is not a man of sense to dispute the road with such an animal.

⇥ Patrick Henry (Precepts Instilled In Him By His Uncle)

To be true & first in all my dealings. To bear no malice nor hatred in my heart. To keep my hands from picking & stealing. Not to covet other men's goods but to learn & labor truly to get my own living & to do my duty in that station of life unto which it shall please God to call me.

⇥ Adam Smith, "The Wealth Of Nations"

The statesman who should attempt to direct private people in what manner they ought to employ their capital would not only load himself with a most unnecessary attention, but assume an authority which could safely be trusted, not only to no single person but to no council or Sen. whatever and which would nowhere be so dangerous as in the hands of a man who had folly & presumption enough to fancy himself fit to exercise it.

❧ Sydney Harris

One way to distinguish truth from all its counter-feits is by its modesty: truth demands only to be heard among others while its counterfeits demand that others be silenced.

❧ James A. Garfield

The men who succeed best in pub. life are those who take the risk of standing by their own convictions.

❧ Dale Carnegie

Any fool can criticize, condemn & complain—& most fools do.

⚸ Mahatma Gandhi

I have not conceived my mission to be that of a knight-errant wandering everywhere to deliver people from different situations. My humble occupation has been to show people how they solve their own difficulties. My work will be finished if I succeed in carrying conviction to the human family, that every man or woman, however weak in body, is the guardian of his or her self respect & liberty. . . . This defense avails through the whole world may be against the individual register.

⚸ Gen. Petain After Fall Of France, WWII

Our spirit of enjoyment was stronger than our spirit of sacrifice. We wanted to have more than we wanted to give. We spared effort and met disaster.

❧ Abe Lincoln

If I were to try to read much less answer all of the attacks made on me, this shop might as well be closed of any other business. I do the very best I know how—the very best I can; & I mean to keep doing so until the end. I the end brings me out alright, what is said against me won't amount to anything. If the end brings me out wrong, 10 angels swearing I was right would make no difference.

❧

Letter to his law partner: Don't let the worship of the past or the confusion of the present interfere with realistic planning for the future.

⚜

Let not him who is houseless pull down the house of another but let him work diligently & build one for himself thus by example insuring that his own shall be safe from violence when built.

⚜

That man can compress the most words into the smallest ideas better than any man I have ever met.

⚜

With public sentiment behind you, anything is possible. Without it, nothing is possible. Therefore, he who influences public sentiment performs a vastly more significant act than he who simply meets statutes.

❧

The time comes upon every public man when it is best for him to keep his lips closed.

❧

I must stand with anybody who stands rt.—stnd. with him while he is rt. & part with him when he is wrong.

⇥ Winston Churchill

It's not enough that we do our best; sometimes we have to do what's required.

⇥ Cicero

44 B.C.—The great affairs of life are not performed by physical strength or activity, or nimbleness of body, but by deliberation, character, expression of opinion. Of these old age is not only not deprived, but as a rule, has them in greater degree.

~⚹~

Do not hold the delusion that your advancement is accomplished by crushing others.

⇥ Seneca

The foundation of true joy is the conscience.

✎ Pericles

A man who takes no interest in public affairs is not a man who minds his own business. We say he has no business being here at all.

✎ Marcus Antonius

Look well unto thyself; there is a source which will always spring up if thou wilt always search there.

✎ Confucius

The interior man seeks what is right; the inferior one what is profitable.

⇥ **Arabian Honey**

In seeking honey expect the sting of bees.

⇥ **Thomas Macaulay**

The measure of a man's real character is what he would do if he knew he would never be found out.

⇥ **Talmud**

Who is wise? He who learns from everybody. Who is strong? He who conquers self. Who is rich? He who is satisfied with what he has. Who is honored? He who is honored by his neighbors.

⇥ **Scotch Ballad**

I am hurt but I am not slain—I'll lie me down & bleed a while & then I'll fight again.

⇥ **Aristotle**

Ed. is the best provision for old age.

⇥ **Leonard Read**

Perfect communication pre-supposes the perfect sayer & the perfect listener, neither one of whom ever existed. Worlds apart? Not necessarily—many are just words apart.

⚜

No bad idea is ever overcome by attacking the persons who believe it.

⚜

Do not argue—first present a better idea.

⚜

Honesty is as much abandoned by the theft of a dime as of a dollar.

⚜

Never concede to a friend any more power over the lives of others than you would to your worst enemy.

❧ Poet Schreiner

Upon the road which you would travel there is no reward offered. Who goes—goes freely for the great love that is in him. The work is his reward.

❧ Proverbs 20:17

The bread of deceit is sweet to a man; but afterward his mouth shall be filled with gravel.

❧ Ecclesiastes 10:12

The words from a wise man's mouth are gracious; but the lips of a fool will swallow up himself.

⇻   Colossians 4:6

Let your speech be always with grace, seasoned with salt, that ye may know how ye ought to answer every man.

⇻   Exodus 20:13 (Cap. Punishment) & 21:12

Thou shalt not kill—He that smiteth a man so that he die shall surely be put to death.

⇻   Spanish Proverb

To reply to an evil word by another taunt is like trying to clean off dirt with mud.

⇥   Pascal

Thought constitutes the greatness of man.

⇥   Anonymous

When we are right we credit our judgment & when we are wrong we blame our luck.

⌘

It is not necessary for all men to be great in action; the greatest & sublimest power is often simple patience.

✒ Gov. Jack Williams—Arizona

Such things as truth, bravery, Loyalty, Honor, Love, kindness are the stars that hang always in the Heavens of all history—we never quite reach them, but as with the stars that used to guide a mariner to safe harbor, they are there for us to guide our conduct by.

✒ "Wanted," Sonnet by J. G. Holland

God give us men! A time like this demands strong minds, great hearts, true faith, and ready hands; men whom the lust of office does not kill! Men whom the spoils of office cannot buy; men who possess opinions & a will, men who have honor; men who will not lie; men who can stand before a demagogue & d—n his treacherous flatteries without winking; tall men, sun crowned, who live above the fog in public duty & in private thinking. For while the rabble with their thumb-worn creeds, their large professions, & their little deeds mingle in selfish strife, lo freedom weeps, wrong rules the land & waiting justice sleeps.

⇥ Anonymous

Charity often consists of a generous impulse to give away something we don't want.

⇥ Viktor Frankl, Austrian Writer

A man who becomes conscious of the responsibility he bears toward a human being who affectionately waits for him or to an unfinished work will never be able to throw away his life. He knows the *why* for his existence and will be able to learn the *how*.

⤝ The Art of Living by Wilfred A. Peterson

Happiness does not depend on what happens outside of you but on what happens inside of you; it is measured by the spirit in which you meet the problems of life. Happiness is a state of mind. Lincoln once said: "We are as happy as we make up our minds to be." Happiness doesn't come from doing what we like to do but from liking what we have to do. Happiness comes from putting our hearts in our work & doing it with joy & enthusiasm. Happiness grows out of harmonious relationship with others based on attitudes of good will, tolerance, understanding & love. The master secret of happiness is to meet the challenge of each new day with the serene faith that "all things work together for good them that love God."

⊰⊱ From "Force 20 from Navarone,"
Alistair Maclean

When all things are lost & there is no hope left, there is always somewhere in this world one man you can turn to. There may be *only* one man. More often than not, there is only one man. But that one man is always there. Or so they say.

⊰⊱ Maxwell Anderson Speaking at
Rutgers U., 1941

The purpose of the theatre is to find & hold up to our regard what is admirable in the human race. The theatrical profession may protest as much as it likes, the theologians may protest and the majority of those who see our plays would probably be amazed to hear it, but the theatre is a religious institution—devoted entirely to the exaltation of the spirit of man. It is an attempt to justify not the ways of God to man but the ways of man to himself. It is an attempt to prove that man has a dignity & and a destiny, that his life is worth living, that he is not purely animal & without purpose. There is no doubt in my mind that our theatre, instead of being as the evangelical ministers used to believe the gateway to h—l, is as much of a worship as the theatre of the Greeks and has exactly the same meaning in our lives The plays that please most and run longest in these sin-haunted alleys (of Broadway) are representative of human loyalty, courage, love that purges the soul, grief that ennobles The great plays of the world . . . teach one & all that an evil action revenges itself upon the doer. "Antigone" & "Hamlet" & 10,000 modern plays argue that injustice is corrosive & will eat the heart out of him who practices it. Analyze any play you please which has survived the test of continued favor & you will find a moral or a rule of social conduct or a rule of thumb which the race has considered valuable enough to learn & pass along. There have been critics who held that the theatre was central among the arts because it is a synthesis of all of them. Now I confess that the theatre appears to me to be the central art—but for a different reason. It does bring together all the arts of a number of them together in a communal religious service. Any other art practiced separately can be either moral or amoral, religious or pagan, affirmative or despairing. But when they come together in the theatre they must affirm, they cannot be detached, they cannot deny. It is as if poetry, music, narration, dancing and the mimetic arts were bits & pieces of theatrical art, stripped away to function alone and rudderless without the moral compulsion of the theatre.

⚜

And now I must give a definition of what seems to me morally sound. If an artist believes that there is good & that there is evil, and in his work favors what seems to him good and expects the ultimate victory for it, then he is morally sound. If he does not believe in the existence of good & evil, or if believing in them, he asks or even anticipates the triumph of evil, he is morally unsound. To some artists the present good may seem evil & the present evil good. That has happened often in the case of a poet or prophet. A playwright cannot run so far ahead of his audience, for he must find a common denominator of his belief in his own generation & even the greatest, the loftiest, must say something which his age can understand. In brief I have found my religion in the theatre where I least expected to find it, & where few will credit that it exists. But it is there, & any man among you who tries to write plays will find himself serving it, if only because he can succeed in no other way. He will discover, if he works through his apprenticeship that the theatre is the central artistic symbol of the struggle of good & evil within men. Its teaching is that the struggle is eternal & unremitting, that the forces which tend to drag men down are always present, always ready to attack, that the forces which make for good cannot sleep through a night without danger.

⇥ M. Anderson Began The Above Lecture With These Words

The story of a play must be the story of what happens within the mind or heart of a man or woman. It cannot deal primarily with external events. The external events are only symbols of what goes on within . . . Excellence on stage is always moral excellence. A struggle on the part of a hero to better his material circumstances is of not interest in a play unless his character is somehow tried in the fire, & unless he comes out of his trial a better man.

⇥ Gilbert K. Chesterton

Loving means to love that which is unlovable or it is not virtue at all; forgiving means to pardon the unpardonable or it is no virtue at all; faith means believing in the unbelievable or it is no virtue at all. And to hope means hoping when things are hopeless or it is no virtue at all.

⊰⊱ **Judge Learned Hand**

Charity is injurious unless it helps the recipient become independent of it.

⤖

Nothing which is morally wrong can ever be politically right.

⤖

One way to settle a disagreement is on the basis of what is right not who is right.

❧ Seneca

He who knows no ports to sail for finds no winds favorable.

❧ George Washington

Let us raise a standard to which the wise & honest can repair.

❧ Wendell Willkie

Let us not tear it asunder. For no man knows when it is destroyed where or when man will find its protective warmth again.

⇥ Marie Montessori

When asked why she didn't reply to her critics replied that if she were climbing a ladder & a dog came yapping at her heels she would have 2 choices. Either she could stop & kick the dog or she could continue to climb the ladder. She preferred to climb.

ON POLITICAL
THEATER

჻

⊰| Rene Wormser, Council for House Spec.
Committee on Tax Exempt Foundation

Research & experimental stations were established at
selected U's, notably Columbia, Stanford, & Chi. Here
some of the worst mischief in recent ed. was born. In
these Rockefeller & Carnegies established vineyards
worked many of the principal characters in the story of
suborning or Am. ed. Here foundations nurtured some
of the most ardent academic advocates of upsetting the

Am. system & supplanting it with a Socialist state. Whatever its earlier origins or manifestations there is little doubt that the radical movement in ed. was accelerated by an organized Socialist movement in the U.S.

⇥ Jack Henning, Exec. California AFL-CIO, Re. R.R.CGOV

Within the past 2 yrs. Gov R. has signed bills increasing soc. insurance benefits for injured and unemployed Calif. workers by more than $266 mil. No Gov. R or D in the history of Calif. has ever done anything like that.

⇥ Sen. McGovern, Inconsistencies of A Liberal

Wash. Post 5/17/72—I have sought not to whip up emotions. There is plenty of anger & tension without our leaders adding to it. I think a conciliatory approach is needed.

Cand. for Pres. McGovern

Wash. Riots—May '71—Well if I were Pres. there wouldn't be demonstrating like that. Those people would be having dinner in the W.H. instead of protesting outside.

⚜

N.Y. Times— 3/19/72—But Henry Jackson destroyed whatever chance he had of becoming the Dem. nominee by embracing racialism in the anti-bussing campaign.

⚜

United Press 4/7/72—Thieu is a corrupt dictator who jails opponents. A despicable creature who doesn't merit the life of a single Am. soldier or for that matter a simple Vietnamese.

Sen. McGovern—When It Was LBJ's War

I support the strafing ordered by Pres. Johnson because I agree when our forces are attacked & our interests are under fire we have to respond with appropriate retaliation.

⚜

N. Vietnam can't benefit anymore than S. Vietnam from a prolonged conflict. I would hope that we would wage such a conflict rather than surrender the area to communism.

A.P. 4/16/72

Pres. Nixon has descended to a new level of bar-
barism & foolhardiness to save his own face and
prop up the corrupt regime of Thieu.

Speech Cath. U. 4/20/72

I think the re-election of Pres. Nixon would be
an open hunting right for this man to give in to
all his impulses for a major war against the people
of Indo-China.

6/29/72 Interview with A.P. Gregg Herrington

I've said many times that the Nixon bombing policy on Indo-China is the most barbaric action that
any country has committed since Hitler's efforts
to exterminate the Jews in Germany in the 30s.

L.A. Times 8/30/72—Re: Reducing Our U.N. Forces by 12,000

Mr. Nixon's policy threatens the men we have remaining there with a grave & growing threat of annihilation. I want to be blunt about it—Nixon's playing pols. with the lives of Am. soldiers & with Am. prisoners rotting in their cells in Hanoi. He's putting his own pol. selfish interests ahead of the W.F. of those young Ams. & of the taxpayers of this country who are bearing the burden.

"Life" 7/7/72 On Death Of J. Edgar Hoover

I could feel nothing but relief that he was no longer a pub. servant.

P. 93 Mcgovern's Biog.

I don't know how Karl Mundt felt about me but I know I hated his guts. I hated him so much I lost my balance.

Cong. Record Sept. 8 1964—P. 21690

I regard Mr. Goldwater as the most unstable, radical & extremist ever to run for the presidency in either pol. party.

⇥ Tax Law

Sec. 351(e)(1) Internal Revenue Code—deals with collapsible corps.—The 1st sentence contains 551 words (Since '76 tax reform act).

⚘

Last sentence of sec. 509(a)(5) of the Code—"For purposes of paragraph 3 an org. described in par. 2 shall be deemed to include an org. described in Section 501(c) 4, 5, or 6 which would be described in par. 2 if it were an org. described in sec. 501(c)(3).

⚜

Inc. tax law was passed in 1914. Since then Dems. have cut the tax once. Repubs. have cut it 14 times. I used this in a speech in 1978. A '78 poll had shown 95% of people rated inflat. as our biggest problem. 81% put high cost of govt. & taxes 2nd. In some poll a majority said Dems. are better at cutting taxes than Republicans.

⇥ Norman Thomas

Our Dem. friends are too Utopian, they promise too much to everyone too easily. Ind. News. Oct. 1960.

⇥ Gov. E. Warren, 1948

Large counties are far more important in the life of our state than their population bears to the entire pop.

of the st. It is for this reason that I have never been in favor of re-distributing representation in our Sen. on a strictly population basis.

⊰ Oct. 1957, "Foreign Affairs"

Sen. J. F. Kennedy urged that we disengage from European conservatives & establish closer liaison with the soc. forces. He declared—"The age of Adenauer is over."

⊰ Dr. John Hannah, Pres. Michigan St.

Speaks out for "Nat. direction of education as a primary instrument of nat. policy."

⇥ **Mr. H. Thomas James, School of Ed. Stanford U.**

As the states have denied, 1st to the family, & then to local communities, the right to make decision on ed. contrary to staff defined policy, so the nation may be expected to deny the states the right to make decisions on educational policy that are not in accord with the *emerging national policy for ed.*

⇥ **Graham Barden (Recently) Chairman, House Ed. & Labor Comm.**

Purpose of Fed. aid bill of '57 was to centralize power over our school system here in Wash. where it is easier to apply concentrated pressure.

HUMOR

⚜

There are 3 kinds of lies: lies, d—m lies, & statistics.

⚜

Those Congressmen who worried about being bugged by the FBI—you'd think they'd be glad someone was listening to them.

❧

Letter addressed to occupant—ever think of sending check back signed occupant.

❧

All for econ. as long as they can spend more money.

❧

Their idea of fighting crime is longer suspended sentences.

❧

Like saying Burton married E. Taylor for her money.

⤟

When operating on a Demo. pol. even the keenest analytic surgeon cannot separate demagogic from solid tissue without killing his patient.

⤟

Fireman boasted he'd caught 20 lb. salmon. Q: "Any witnesses?" A: "If there weren't . . . would have weighed 40 lbs."

⤟

Simple diet—if it tastes good spit it out.

⁓❦⁓

Economist is a fellow who takes long steps to save his new $10 shoes & splits his $20 slacks.

⁓❦⁓

Some people try to be so broadminded they wind up just shallow.

⁓❦⁓

Every time the govt. shifts to the left the decimal point in taxes shifts to the right.

⁓❦⁓

Some tasks have to be put off a doz. times before they slip your mind.

꧁

When all the cars in the city are laid end to end it's a weekend.

꧁

Ignorance can't be bliss or a lot of people would be jumping up & down with joy.

꧁

If you wrote 9 people today & each of them wrote to 9 diff. people tomorrow & this continued for just 10 days—you'd reach 3,486,784,401.

✤

Upper crust . . . lot . . . old crumbs held together by dough.

✤

To err is human—it takes a computer to really louse things up.

✤

Many foxes grow grey but few grow good.

✤

Worst wheel on the wagon makes the most noise.

❧

An empty bag cannot stand upright.

❧

Could say horse in 9 langs. but bought a cow to ride on.

❧

Tricks are the prac. of fools who haven't the wit to be honest.

❧

He who scatters thorns should not go barefoot.

❦

Confidence—what you start out with before . . . understand . . . situation.

❦

Newest thing in women's hairdos is men.

❦

Some people are so addicted to exaggeration they can't tell the truth without lying.

❦

Husband: "In our 6 yrs. marriage we haven't been able to agree on anything." Wife: "It's been 7 yrs., dear."

⚜

Inflation—changed . . . pumpernickel bread to pumperdime.

⚜

There is a noble forgetfulness—that which does not remember injuries.

⚜

Voltaire: "In general the art of govt. consists of taking as much money as poss. from one class of citizens to give to the other."

⚜

We are all aware that "moderation" is a good rule for health—exercise moderately, eat the same way—drink in moderation but moderation should be taken in moderation. For example—should a man be moderately faithful to wife? How about your banker—is he moderately honest? That school bus driver—moderately good driver? Somehow I hope the plane I take to L.A. is more than moderately safe. How about in the operating room—the man with the scalpel in his hand—does he have a moderately good record of success with this type of op.? Have you met your son's fiancée—she insists she's a moderately virtuous young woman.

⚜

We all want our sons to have all the things we never had when we were their age—especially a report card with a lot of "A"s.

⌘

Lady Driver: The thing I dislike about parking is the noisy crash.

⌘

Latest from Moscow—someone just broke into the Kremlin and stole next year's election results.

⌘

Some people are so indecisive their favorite color is plaid.

⌘

News Item: Rep. Mario Briggs' used . . . Cong. Rec. for a glowing testimonial to his N.Y. colleague Frank

Brasco. Heaping praise on Brasco that his fellow Dem. had decided to retire. He didn't mention that Brasco will be sentenced to Fed. prison this month for bribery.

⌘

Conscience is that still small voice that tells you when you are about to get caught.

⌘

Fishing is something you should do yesterday when they were biting.

⌘

MAN AT TESTIMONIAL DINNER: 47 years ago I walked into this town with my earthly pos-sessions tied in a red bandana on a stick. This

town has been good to me—I'm on the board
of the bank, own 2 apt. buildings & an office
building and have branch businesses in 39 cities.

LITTLE BOY: Sir, what was in that bandana 47
years ago?

MAN: $300,000 cash.

⚜

You know why it's called horse sense—they don't bet
on people.

⚜

Technology—what makes it take less time to cross the
ocean & longer to drive to work.

❦

Old fellow: Yep I'm 94 and haven't got an enemy in the world—last one petered out about a yr. ago.

❦

Ask an atheist who's just had a great meal if he believes there's a cook.

❦

If all the cans in the world were placed end to end some dope would pull out & try to pass them.

❦

A protest march is like a tantrum only better organized.

❦

The trouble with staying home from work is that you have to drink coffee on your own time.

❦

Beware of those who fall at your feet. They may be reaching for the corner of the rug.

❦

Some people want to check govt. spending & some people want to spend govt. checks.

❦

Today if someone offered us the world on a silver platter most of us would take the platter.

⛥

Money may not buy friends but it will help you to stay in contact with your children.

⛥

As long as there are final exams there will be prayer in schools.

⛥

Flattery is what makes husbands of bachelors.

⛥

New credit plan: "Try our easy payment plan, 100% down & nothing to pay."

❧

Conscience is that still small voice that tells you what other people should do.

❧

Don't mind going to work . . . that long wait til quitting time.

❧

Sometimes if you have a good idea tell it to someone else for about ¾ hour until he thinks it's his. Then when he subsequently brings it up express doubt & finally reluctantly agree to sign it or try it on an experimental basis. There is nothing like skepticism to gain support for an idea.

❦

Seen a pacemaker with more compassion.

❦

Spks. with all the authority of an empty podium.

❦

Wife cheering up depressed husband: What do you mean nothing to live for—house isn't pd. for, car isn't pd. for, washing machine, TV. . .

❦

Nice thing about long range goals—you don't get frustrated with short range failures.

⚜

That dumb blonde in the office may turn out to be a smart brunette.

⚜

Clover leaf—something mks. it possible to drive someplace didn't intend to go.

⚜

Insanity is hereditary—get it from your children.

⚜

Govt. programs like old soldiers never die—but neither do they fade away.

⤪

Roughly you can divide people into 2 classes—those who still possess the fierce hunting instinct & those who pay to park their cars.

⤪

A smart husband knows exactly the right thing to say when he quarrels with . . . wife but if he's really smart he doesn't say it.

⤪

And now a man who needs no intro.—he didn't show up.

⁓❦⁓

Man who changed Drs. told a friend the new one had him on iron tablets, iron shots, and a once a month intravenous iron injection. "And you feel better?" "Only when I'm facing north."

⁓❦⁓

The farmer slowed down [at the] Dr.'s orders—couldn't pay the Dr.—lost the farm.

⁓❦⁓

Baseball rookie—catcher talk—pitcher: "never mind I've pitched to this guy before"—catcher: "I know—in this inning."

⋙

The good years—when the kids were old enough to cut the grass & too young to drive the car.

⋙

Used to tlk. out prices over cig. & coffee—now cigs. and coffee are our prob.

⋙

Adolescent kid—old enough . . . dress self . . . cn. only remember where dropped clothes.

⋙

Good judgment comes from exp. & exp. comes . . . poor judgment.

꽃

Before TV no one knew what a headache looked like.

꽃

Why can't life's problems hit us when we're 18 and know everything.

꽃

Easier to forgive someone if you get even with him first.

꽃

This country needs some colleges to teach everything the students think they know.

❦

Most people's financial problems are very simple—they are short of money.

❦

It's not cheaper car that people want—it's an expensive car that costs less.

❦

Daytime TV—that's a punishment employers have come up with for workers who stay home when they're not really sick.

❦

The hardest decision in life is when to start middle age.

⤞⤝

Gypsy fortune teller: "You'll be poor & unhappy until you are 40." And what then? "Nothing—then you'll be used to it."

⤞⤝

Never start an argument with a woman when she's tired—or when she's rested.

⤞⤝

Won't say he should be put in a mental inst. but if he was in one—don't think I'd let him out.

Room bugged? every time I sneezed the chandelier said Gesundheit.

Time you *enjoy* wasting is not wasted time.

Work hard and save your money and when you are old you can afford the things only young people can enjoy.

There are no *new* sins—old ones are just getting better publicity.

⤞

Don't close saloons—elec. day any more too many candies.—getting locked in.

⤞

Influence is what you think you have until you try to use it.

⤞

Poise is looking like an owl after behaving like a jackass.

⚜

All the recipes for success have some ingredients—for nervous brk. down—it's the amt. of each & the way you mix them that makes the diff.

⚜

Big difficulty is [in] cutting down govt. expense is the expenses have votes.

⚜

Absent minded patient went to dr. for a check up— got a handwritten prescription—put in a billfold & forgot to get it filled. Every morning 2 yrs showed it to conductor as a RR pass, 2x got him into a the-atre—once a ballgame. Got a raise by showing it to the cashier as a note from the boss. One day laid it down—his daughter played it on the piano & won a scholarship to the Am. Conservatory. He used it to get to her 1st concert.

⚜

Henry Etienne 1531–98—"si jeunesse savior, si viellesse pouvoit" If only youth had the knowledge—if only age had the strength.

⚜

Can't stand someone talking while he's interrupting.

⚜

If at 1st don't succeed, don't try Russian Roulette.

❧

If at 1st don't succeed, get a h—l lot advice.

❧

Could read "Making of the Pres." & not know the ending.

❧

Finally learned to smash the atom—should have given it to the P.O.—smashed everything else.

❧

If Geo. W. never told a lie what's his pic. doing on a 39 cent $1.00 bill.

⁓⁓⁓

Don't know whether they'll cure poverty but they sure cured wealth.

⁓⁓⁓

Man's home is his castle—looks like a home but it's taxed like a castle.

⁓⁓⁓

Don't mind govt's. war on pov. But use our money for ammo.

⁓⁓⁓

He has all the charm of a dirty Xmas card.

✧

Hippie keeps stealing his mother's beads—she hopes he's a hippie.

✧

3 wise men on an island told vast tidal wave soon destroy and totally cover island. 1st would take family to highest pt. & spend last hours in meditation and prayer. 2nd live it up and try to experience ultimate pleasures. 3rd surround self with best advisors could find & learn to live under water.

✧

Tom Edison asked if he considered work a wasted effort after 28,000 unsuccessful exper. on a new type battery. "No—now know 28,000 things won't work."

꧁

Man had nite mares every nite—big savage animals crawled out from under bed & attacked him. "Went to my brother and he stopped it." "You're brother is a psych.?" "No—carpenter—he sawed the legs off the bed."

꧁

Today—plenty of buffalo and the trains are nearly extinct.

꧁

Cooking a TV dinner doesn't put you in show business.

⚜

Muggers picketing—want more parks.

⚜

There is a legend among snakes that once upon a time a mama & a papa snake living in the garden of Eden were corrupted by humans.

⚜

I used to think I was poor. Then they tell me I was needy. They said I was being self defeating—I wasn't needy—I was culturally deprived. Then they said deprived was a bad image—I was underprivileged. That became overused and I became disadvatanged. I still don't have a dime but I do have a great vocabulary.

⚜

You'll always stay young if you live honestly, eat slowly, sleep sufficiently, work industriously, worship faithfully and lie about your age.

⚜

Anyone who thinks he's going to be happy and prosperous by letting govt. take care of him should take a good look at the Am. Indian.

⚜

Saw a chimp—could sort photos of apes and humans. Humans on one pile—apes on the other. But every time she came to her own pic. she put in on the pile with the humans.

❧

Mama Bear to Papa Bear: This is positively my last year as a den mother.

❧

We are already working a 4 day week—it just takes 5 or 6 to do it.

❧

You don't have to be awake nights to succeed—just stay awake days.

❧

A sweater—that's something your kid wears when his mother feels chilly.

꒜

My son is studying Eng.—now he talks back with perfect diction.

꒜

Police sent out pics. of an escaped convict in 6 dif. poses—A small town constable sent wire . . . have captured 5 of them & on the trail of the 6th.

꒜

Managing ed. to cub reporter—"names are essential in every story" Cub handed in story—"Last night lightening struck a barn n.w. of town—3 cows were killed—Rosie, Isabel & Mabel."

⌘

Pilot to control tower—"I'm coming in please give me landing instructions"—tower to pilot—"why are you yelling so loud?"—Pilot—"I don't have a radio."

⌘

Adolescence is the time when children suddenly feel responsible for answering the phone.

⌘

If at 1st you don't succeed, do it the way she told you.

⌘

A compliment may be blunt, but criticism calls for courtesy.

❦

Prosperity is something created by businessmen for politicians to take credit for.

❦

Mod. styles—buckle shoes, loafers, moccasins. A man can earn his Ph.D. without learning to tie his shoelace.

❦

Teacher asked kid what he did to care for his teeth— "watch out for kids who shove at the drinking fountain."

❧

Inflation—that's the price we pay for those govt. benefits everybody thought were free.

❧

What with a major flu epidemic & a bad snow storm, Wash. D.C. was in a bad way. Reporter doing a story on the sit. called a big govt. agency to see how it had been affected. The asn. he got revealed more than intended. A cheerful voice said "we're functioning normally—with only 1/2 our staff"

❧

Sam Levinson raised in a tenement says "never knew my family was underprivileged. We thought we slept 5 in a bed because it was more fun that way"

⁓❧⁓

There is nothing wrong with them that trying to reason with them won't aggravate.

⁓❧⁓

Neighbor asked a little boy how many children in the family. "Seven." My that must cost a lot. "Oh no—we don't buy 'em—we raise 'em."

⁓❧⁓

Govt.—like—brassiere—oppresses—opulent—uplifts—fallen & deceives—unwary.

Can't beat the logic of a fisherman when he wants to stay at it another few hours. One reason of course is because the fish are biting—the other is because they aren't.

Albert was so slow in learning to talk his parents thought he was abnormal. His teacher called him a misfit and his classmates avoided him. He failed his 1st college entrance exam—Albert's last name was Einstein.

If you get up earlier in the morning than your neighbor—work harder—scheme more & stick to the job more closer—stay up later planning to get ahead—

you'll leave more money when you die & you'll leave it a lot sooner.

⌘

Bathtub—invented in 1850—phone in 1875—for 25 years you could have a sit in the tub without having the phone ring.

⌘

After a traffic accident, one woman rushed out of the crowd to lean over one of the victims. She was roughly pushed aside by a fellow who said "stay back—I've had a course in 1st aid." The woman stood—watched the mans ministrations for a few mins. then tapped him on the shoulder—she said, "when you get to the part about calling the Dr.—I'm already here."

✧

A bargain sale—where women fight for things that have been reduced in price because no one wanted them in the 1st place.

✧

Today the average man lives 25 yrs. longer than he did a century ago—he has to—to get his taxes paid.

✧

The good old days—took your horse to a blacksmith—he put shoes on it and didn't tell you a dozen other things you ought to have done to it.

⚜

Taxpayers—that's someone who doesn't have to pass a civil service exam to work for the govt.

⚜

Housewife just has to reverse things these days—fill the shopping cart with money & put the groceries in her purse.

⚜

Some instead of trying to drown their troubles take them out and give them swimming lessons.

⌘

Judge: "Your age madam?"—"30 years"—J: "You may have a hard time proving that"—"You'll have a hard time proving that I'm not—the court house where my birth was registered burned down in 1920."

⌘

Man took his son to visit Cong.—Boy asked "who is that man at the platform?"—"Chaplain"—"Does he pray for the members?"—"No—when he goes into the house & sees the members—he prays for the country."

⌘

Russian & Am. arguing about freedom. Am said "You don't understand in my country I can walk up to the White House and go to the Pres. office, bang on his desk and say 'Jerry Ford I don't like the way you're running my country."—Russian: "I can do the same thing. I can go to the Kremlin walk up to Brezhnev, bang on his desk and say 'I don't like the way Jerry F. is running his country.'"

⚜

Young man—Pol: "I wouldn't vote for you if you were St. Peter. "Pol: "If I were St. Peter you wouldn't vote for me—you wouldn't be in my district."

⚜

With metric conversion upon us—of one thing I'd like to be sure: are 28,349 grams of prevention worth .453 kilograms of cure.

❧

You know they've been watching too much TV when a kid: "Mommy, I like you better than any other leading brand."

❧

Your wife used to be so nervous!" "She's fine now—the Dr. told her nervousness was a sign of old age."

❧

Any man who thinks he is more intel. than his wife is married to a very smart woman.

꧁

Middle age—when you begin exchanging emotions for symptoms.

꧁

People who live in glass houses might as well answer the doorbell.

꧁

Glad to pay as we go if we could ever get caught up paying for where we've been.

꧁

When a woman loves a man he can get her to do most anything she really wants to.

⚜

Cop: "Said to myself when you came around the corner 45 at least." Woman: Oh this dress always makes me look 5 yrs. older.

⚜

Door—Nats.Cap—"Genl. Svcs. Admin Region 3 Pub Bldg. Scv. Bldg. Mngmnt. Div. Utility Rm. Custodial"—Broom Closet

⚜

Weary real estate man—spent all day Sun. showing a couple the model homes—finally in about the 10th model home—"here is the hobby room—do you folks have any hobbies?"—Wife—"Yes—looking the model homes on Sundays."

꧁

The condition of a man can be judged by what he takes 2 at a time—stairs or pills.

꧁

The best sub. for experience is being 17 yrs. old.

꧁

Coliseum in Rome—tour guide, "this is room where the slaves dressed to fight the lions." Woman, "But how does someone dress to fight lions?"—T.G.—"Very slowly."

❧

Country Dr. parked his old jalopy while he called on a patient. Came back to kids around the corner laughing and making fun of it. He said "It's paid for." Then looking at the kids—said you're not, you're not. . .

❧

Women can't do without marriage—who'll steady the step ladder while they're painting the ceiling?

❧

I won't say their marriage is unhappy but he went down to the marriage license bureau to see if the license had expired.

⚜

An old French soldier after the battle Verdun: "there are no hopeless situations, There are only men & wm. who've grown hopeless about them."

⚜

Convict blamed all his problems, on his lawyer—says he kept demanding the jury give him justice & they did.

⚜

An underdeveloped Nation—that's one Henry Kissinger hasn't visited yet.

⁓❦⁓

Camp director told a mother he'd have to discipline her son. She said well don't be too hard—he's very sensitive—slap the boy next to him & that'll scare Irving.

⁓❦⁓

A young poet who had just sold his 1st verse walking—very despondent. Friend: "What is the matter?" Poet: "Shakespeare is dead—Keats, Shelly, Byron—all are dead. The responsibility on my shoulders is almost more than I can bear."

⁓❦⁓

Rec'd letter "You have no guts"—A Friend

⁓

A cit. filed a claim for Medicare payment—a dozen letters & months later found out why no payment— Soc. Security told him he'd passed away.

⁓

Nothing in life is so exhilarating as to be shot at without result—Churchill

⁓

Sgt. "Put a pair of clean socks on every day"—end of the week the recruit couldn't get his shoes on.

RONALD REAGAN

✤

Politics—got so expensive—takes—lot—money just to get beat.

✤

It's not our pub. men can't put your finger on, so it's our pub. We are only fleas weighing over 100 lbs. We don't know what we want, but we are ready to bite somebody to get it.

✤

I'll bet you—time ain't far off when a woman won't know anymore than a man.

✧

Only in a country where it takes you more intel. to fig. out your inc. tax than it takes to earn the inc.

✧

If a rabbit foot is lucky—how come it didn't work for the rabbit.

✧

Elderly motorist going down 1 way street—Cop: "Do you know where you're going?"—"No," the old fellow admitted, "but I must be late because everyone else is coming back."

Cong. biggest job—how to get money from the tax-payer without disturbing the water.

3 ways to get something done: Do it yourself—have someone else do it—or forbid your kids to do it.

Costrophobia—the fear of rising prices.

Today's kids are studying in hist. what we studied in current events.

⚜

Human Nature—That's what makes it easier to break a commandment than a habit.

⚜

Mess Segt. "The men of Valley Forge would have loved this." Soldier—"Sure, it was fresh then."

⚜

Guest arrived—tiptoed in without knocking—sat silently etc, Finally one mentioned the note on the door. She'd forgotten was taking a nap & left a note for her children. "Door is unlocked. Come in quietly—no rough housing—don't ask for anything & if you touch the food on the table I'll skin you alive."

❧

Texas even claims Geo. W. was a Texan. Story is he cut down a cactus—his father said Geo. did you cut that cactus down. Geo. whimpered I cannot tell a lie—I did it with my little hatchet. His father yelled—if you can't tell a better story—get out.

❧

Our problem is a lack of movies that are rated E for entertainment.

❧

The younger gen. has no faults that being a parent & a taxpayer will not eliminate.

꧁

There's little danger of our govt. being overthrown—
there's too much of it.

꧁

If you dread getting old because you wont be able to
do the things you want to do—don't worry when you
get older you won't want to do them.

꧁

Prices are so high you don't order a chuck roast anymore—you have to call it Charles.

⚜

A fellow with one of those foreign jobs—"Fill'er up"—Stuck hose in tank—finally said—"Better shut off the engine Mr.—you're gaining on me."

⚜

Tchr.—"What was the great diff. Geo. W. had to face?" Kid—"He couldn't tell a lie."

⚜

Guests for dinner—mother asked 4 yr. old to say the blessing—he said "Don't know what say." She: "Just say what you heard me say"—Kid, bowed his head: "Oh Lord why did I invite these people here on a hot day like this."

⁓⁋⁓

Adam and Eve must have been Russian—they had no roof over their heads, nothing to wear, only one apple between them & they called it paradise.

⁓⁋⁓

Income tax—it's a fine for reckless thriving.

⁓⁋⁓

Communication—a fellow in a cafe to waiter: "I can't eat my soup." "Sorry I'll call the mgr." (same line) "I'll call the chef." (same line)—"what's the matter with it?"—"No spoon."

❦

He worshipped the ground she walked on—about 35 acres of downtown Dallas.

❦

If the IRS had to give money back if we weren't satisfied we might get better govt.

❦

We work ourselves to death buying labor saving appliances.

❦

It's easy to forgive an enemy if you know you can lick him.

꿎

People who tell you never let the little things bother you never tried sleeping with a mosquito in the room.

꿎

Good boss takes a little more than his share of the blame and little less than his share of the credit.

꿎

A desk is a wastebasket with drawers.

꿎

Rookie policeman in exam—asked how he would break up a crowd—"take up a collection."

✧

Nothing like a vote in the U.N. to tell you who your friends used to be.

✧

Increase in crime may be from want of pinching (not the pinch of want).

✧

Muskie-Lincoln image. Wearing same suit. He & his pants never seem to sit down at the same time. When se sits his pants are already sitting there waiting for him.

✧

U.S. like Santa Claus—both leave gifts all over the world & wind up holding the bag.

✧

Most people would be glad to mind their own business if the govt. would give it back.

✧

Campaign poster should read "Caution voting for this man may be hazardous to your health, wealth, & welfare."

The art of politics is making people like you no matter what it costs them.

❦

People who think a tax boost will cure inflation are the same ones who believe another drink will cure a hangover.

❦

Bible says "ask & it shall be given." Govt. says the same thing only Govt. has to take it away from someone else first.

⤖

Keeping a budget balanced is a lot like preserving virtue—you have to learn to say "no."

⤖

A bird in the hand is worth 2 in the bush but it's messier.

⤖

Govt. is the wold's 2nd oldest prof. but it has a lot in common with the first—both solicit money & you get just about the same thing for it.

❧

Father waking son—"Get up! When A. Lincoln was your age do you know what he was doing?" Son: "No but I know what he was doing when he was your age."

❧

1st grader: Why does Daddy bring all that paper in his briefcase? Mom: Because he has so much to do at the office he can't finish it all. 1st grader: Why don't they put him in a slower group?

❧

Some of us would like to know if a teacher can hit a child on the hands with a ruler. I say she doesn't have the right to—Maria. P.S. If my writing's bad it's because my hand is sore.

꧁

You are doing a terrific & outstanding job—I'm proud you were elected Gov. of Ohio. This proves anybody can be elected.

꧁

I am going to loose a tooth. My tchr. wants to pull it. I wont let her. I like it where it is—Nancy

꧁

My daddy says since you became Gov. many things have changed. 2 ice cream men used to come down our street but not any more. One of the trucks was pulled by a horse. Did you take him to a racetrack or just change the streets they go down?

﷽

Hywy. Dept.—signs be 7ft. above highway instead of 5. Raised signs at tremendous cost. Fed govt. would have lowered the pavement.

﷽

Magician—boy on stage—"never hv. seen you before"—"no daddy"

﷽

If money could talk—ask "what happened?"

﷽

Good exec. never puts off till tomorrow what . . . can get someone else to do today.

⚜

Hold up man—note—teller "Got gun give money."
She wrote "Kindly go to next window I'm on my lunch
hour."

⚜

Play both ends against the taxpayer.

⚜

When come to parting of the ways—try to go both.

⚜

Practice pols. so that all paths of glories lead but to
the gravy.

⤳❧⤳

He is usually mistaken at the top of his voice.

⤳❧⤳

Man of few words—never stops talking after he's used them.

⤳❧⤳

The main prob. with teenagers is they are just like their parents were at that age.

⤳❧⤳

Want some free newspaper publicity? Do something stupid.

꧁

They went beyond the call of duty—they wanted to get someplace where they couldn't hear it.

꧁

Woman home with pckg. Husband: "what did you buy?" W: "I don't know what it is." H: "Then why did you buy it?" W: "Because the man said you can't get them anymore."

꧁

Heard of a man still has 1st $? This man has stock he bought when the company's name was "General Candle."

❧

Went for singing lessons said—"Don't know what to do with my hands when I sing." Have you tried holding them over your mouth.

❧

U. Prof. of Eng. told class he'd found one of the most elegant lines of poetry in the Eng. language. "Walk with light" (repeat). "Isn't that a wonderful thing to say to someone?" Class agreed & asked who was . . . poet. Prof: "Anonymous . . . it's written on a sign at the corner of 9th & Main."

❧

Visiting friend asked wealth, soc. leader why he stayed in such a small one horse town. He said: "Because I'm the horse."

⋙

Tchr: "Not only is he the worst behaved kid in school—he has a perfect attendance record."

⋙

Things could be worse—100 mil. Ams. don't have driver's licenses.

GLOSSARY

Acton, John Dalberg (1834–1902): English historian with an interest in the American federal system. His extensive library was given to the University of Cambridge.

Adams, Samuel (1722–1803): Second cousin to John Adams, politician in colonial Massachusetts, and one of the Founding Fathers of the United States.

Adams, John (1735–1826): Assisted in drafting the Declaration of Independence. He was the second president of the United States, as well as a political theorist.

Aesop (620–564 BCE): Greek slave and storyteller whose well-known fables, like "The Boy Who Cried Wolf," are often used in the moral education of children.

Amiel, Henri Frédéric (1821–1881): Swiss poet and philosopher who traveled widely and taught moral philosophy in Geneva. He is known for his book *Journal Intime*.

Anderson, Maxwell (1888–1959): American playwright, poet, and author who founded the Playwrights' Company.

Antonius, Marcus (c. 83–30 BCE): Roman politician and general who supported Julius Caesar as military commander, started the Final War of the Roman Republic, and took Cleopatra as his lover.

Aptheker, Herbert (1915–2003): American Marxist historian and political activist who most notably researched African-American history.

Aristotle (384–322 BCE): Greek philosopher, student of Plato, and teacher to Alexander the Great. With Socrates and Plato, one of the founders of Western philosophy.

Barden, Graham (1896–1967): Democratic U.S. congressman from North Carolina. He served thirteen consecutive terms in the House and chaired the House Education Committee and, later, the Education and Labor Committee.

Bastiat, Claude-Frédéric (1801–1850): French liberal theorist, member of the French assembly, and political economist known for his clever attacks on policies enacted by states to protect themselves.

Benton, William (1900–1973): U.S. senator from Connecticut and publisher of the *Encyclopaedia Britannica*. Active organizer of the United Nations.

Booth, William (1829–1912): British Methodist preacher and the founder and first general of the Salvation Army, then an evangelist organization that turned humanitarian.

Browning, Robert (1812–1889): Acclaimed Victorian poet and playwright known for his dramatic monologues. He influenced later poets with his method of building emotional sympathy for unsavory moral characters.

Burke, Edmund (1729–1797): Irish philosopher, statesman, author, and orator known for supporting the American Revolution and opposing the French Revolution, as well as founding the philosophies of modern conservatism.

Carnegie, Dale (1888–1955): American lecturer and author of self-improvement, sales, and business books such as *How to Win Friends and Influence People*.

Chambers, Whittaker (1901–1961): American writer and editor. Once a Communist Party USA member and Soviet spy, he later renounced communism and testified in the perjury and espionage trial of Alger Hiss.

Chesterton, Gilbert (1874–1936): English writer who critiqued both conservatism and liberalism. He also wrote fantasy and detective fiction.

Churchill, Winston (1874–1965): British politician who served as the prime minister of the United Kingdom and led the Allied forces to victory in World War II. He was known for his oratorical skills and his wartime leadership.

Cicero, Marcus (106–43 BCE): Roman theorist, linguist, and translator who introduced Romans to the schools of Greek philosophy. His correspondences with his friend Atticus introduced to Europe the art of letter writing.

Conant, James (1893–1978): Chemist, government official, and president of Harvard University. He was known for reforming Harvard and making it a world-class institution.

Confucius (551–479 BCE): Chinese social philosopher who emphasized morality in all worldly relationships. His teachings are found in the *Analects of Confucius*.

Coolidge, Calvin (1872–1933): Thirtieth president of the United States, succeeding upon the death of Warren G. Harding in 1923. He was controversial for his downsizing of government programs and promotion of laissez-faire economics.

Cotton, John (1585–1652): Core member of the New England Puritan ministers who was influential in shaping church structure and rules.

Denning, Alfred "Tom" (1899–1999): British soldier, lawyer, judge, and mathematician. He became King's Counsel in 1938 and campaigned against the common-law principle of precedent.

Emerson, Ralph Waldo (1803–1882): American poet, lecturer, and transcendentalist who championed freedom and explored the spiritual relationship between man and the world.

Frankl, Viktor (1905–1997): Austrian psychiatrist and

Holocaust survivor who wrote the bestselling book *Man's Search for Meaning*.

Fulbright, J. William (1905–1995): U.S. senator who represented Arkansas. As a Southern Democrat, he opposed the House Un-American Activities Committee and established an international exchange program that now bears his name.

Gandhi, Mahatma (1869–1948): "Father" of India, an honorific applied to him because he politically and ideologically led the movement for India's independence from England. He advocated a particular method of civil disobedience known as *satyagraha*.

Garfield, James (1831–1881): Major general in the Civil War and the twentieth president of the United States. He accomplished very little during his 200 days in office, and he was assassinated on July 2, 1881.

Gladstone, William (1809–1898): British liberal statesman and scholar of Homer, known for his four terms as prime minister and his famous feud with Conservative leader Benjamin Disraeli.

Goebbels, Joseph (1897–1945): German politician and minister of propaganda in Nazi Germany. He was the architect of the *Kristallnacht* attack on German Jews that precipitated the genocide, and he was famous for his oratorical skills.

Gompers, Samuel (1850–1924): English-born leader of the American labor movement. He founded the American Federation of Labor and worked to raise wages for workers.

Gromyko, Andrey (1909–1989): Soviet statesman through the Cold War. He was responsible for much of Soviet foreign policy, including the arms limitations treaties.

Hamilton, Alexander (1755–1804): Founding father and economist. He wrote most of the *Federalist Papers* and was the first U.S. secretary of the treasury. He died in a duel with Aaron Burr.

Hand, Billings Learned (1872–1961): United States judge and judicial philosopher who served on the District Court for the Southern District of New York and the U.S. Court of Appeals for the Second Circuit. He is often quoted for his elegant legal thought.

Hannah, John (1902–1991): President of Michigan State College (now Michigan State University) for twenty-eight years. He later became the head of the United States Agency for International Development (USAID).

Harris, Sydney (1917–1986): American journalist for the *Chicago Daily News* and the *Chicago Sun-Times*. His column, "Strictly Personal," was widely syndicated in North America.

Henning, Jack (1915–2009): Former U.S. ambassador and undersecretary of labor. He was a defender of the minimum wage and civil rights.

Henry, Patrick (1736–1799): Founding Father and leading anti-Federalist, he served as the first and sixth governor of Virginia. He is best remembered for the speech in which he said, "Give me liberty or give me death."

Hill, Benjamin (1823–1882): U.S. representative and senator as well as Confederate senator for the state of Georgia during the Civil War. He was one of few prewar politicians to achieve postwar success.

Hitler, Adolf (1889–1945): Austrian-born German

politician who was appointed chancellor of Germany and transformed it into a fascist state. He is responsible for the Holocaust and the outbreak of World War II.

Holland, Josiah Gilbert (1819–1881): American novelist and poet who wrote under the pseudonym "Timothy Titcomb."

Holmes, Oliver Wendell (1841–1935): American jurist who served as associate justice of the Supreme Court from 1902 to 1932. He was known for being one of the most influential common-law judges, with efforts to support New Deal regulations.

Hoover, Herbert (1874–1964): Thirty-first president of the United States. He was a mining engineer and author who served as the secretary of commerce. As president he unsuccessfully tried to combat the Great Depression.

Hoover, J. Edgar (1895–1972): First director and instrumental founder of the Federal Bureau of Investigation. His controversial tenure led to the instatement of ten-year term limitations for FBI directors.

Hutchins, Robert (1899–1977): Educational philosopher, dean of Yale Law School, and president of the University of Chicago.

Ibn Khaldoun (1332–1406): North African polymath whose expertise lay in astronomy, economics, history, law, and nutrition. He is considered the father of the social sciences, particularly in the East.

Jefferson, Thomas (1743–1826): Third president of the United States, Founding Father, and the principal author of the Declaration of Independence. He promoted republicanism and is consistently ranked among the greatest U.S. presidents.

Johnson, Hiram (1866–1945): American progressive who served as the twenty-third governor of California and later as a U.S. senator. He became a staunch isolationist, opposing the League of Nations and the United Nations.

Kennedy, John F. (1917–1963): Thirty-fifth president of the United States. He was beloved during his short presidency and presided over the Bay of Pigs invasion, the Cuban missile crisis, the space race, and the beginnings of the African-American civil rights movement. He was assassinated in 1963.

Khrushchev, Nikita (1894–1971): Leader of the Soviet Union during parts of the Cold War, including the Cuban missile crisis. He was responsible for the partial de-Stalinization and liberalization of domestic policy in the Soviet Union.

Krock, Arthur (1886–1974): American journalist and Washington correspondent for the *New York Times*. Three-time Pulitzer Prize winner and recipient of the Presidential Medal of Freedom.

Lenin (Vladimir Ilich Ulyanov, 1870–1924): Russian Marxist revolutionary and Communist politician. He led the October Revolution of 1917 and fought to establish a socialist economic system and maintain Communist control through the Russian Civil War.

Lewis, C. S. (1898–1963): Irish-born British novelist and Christian theologian. He is best known for his children's fiction, especially *The Chronicles of Narnia*.

Lieber, Francis (1800–1872): German-American political theorist and jurist. He is widely known as the author of the *Lieber Code*—a code of conduct for troops during wartime—during the American Civil War.

Lincoln, Abraham (1809–1865): Sixteenth president of the United States. He issued the Emancipation Proclamation, freeing slaves, in 1863; led the nation through the Civil War; and was assassinated in April 1865.

Lippmann, Walter (1889–1974): American reporter, commentator, and intellectual who introduced the concept of the Cold War and was twice awarded the Pulitzer Prize for his news column, "Today and Tomorrow."

Macaulay, Thomas (1800–1859): British poet and Whig politician who wrote extensively on British history and served as secretary of war from 1839 to 1841.

MacLean, Alistair (1922–1987): Scottish novelist who wrote thrillers and adventure stories under the pseudonym "Ian Stuart."

Madison, James (1751–1836): Fourth president of the United States and principal drafter of the U.S. Constitution. He was a Founding Father whose belief in individual liberty led to the Bill of Rights. He worked closely with George Washington to establish the new federal government.

Magee, John Gillespie, Jr. (1922–1941): Anglo-American aviator and poet who served in the Royal Canadian Air Force and died in a midair collision during World War II.

Mao Zedong (1893–1976): Han Chinese revolutionary and Communist who led the People's Republic of China from its establishment in 1949 until his death. His political strategies are collectively known as Maoism, and he is said to have laid the foundations for modern China. Because his social and political programs also cost millions of Chinese lives, his legacy is controversial.

Marshall, Henry (1954–): National Football League athlete who played for the Kansas City Chiefs from 1976 to 1987.

McCracken, Paul (1915–): American economist who chaired the President's Council of Economic Advisors under President Nixon and attempted to curb inflation. He now teaches at the University of Michigan.

McCulloch, John Ramsay (1789–1864): Leading Scottish economist in the Ricardian school. He was an early advocate of advanced statistical analysis and the publication of economic data.

McGovern, George (1922–): Historian and former U.S. representative, senator, and Democratic presidential nominee. He lost badly to Richard Nixon in the 1972 presidential election. He has since served as ambassador to the U.N. on World Hunger and was named 2008 World Food Prize Laureate.

Mill, John Stuart (1806–1873): British philosopher and author of *On Liberty*, a hugely influential work on the limits of power and the importance of self-government.

Montessori, Maria (1870–1952): Italian educator and philosopher best known for her unique Montessori method of education, which gives children more freedom and self-direction than conventional education.

Montesquieu (Charles-Louis de Secondat) (1689–1755): French political philosopher known for his articulation of the separation of powers and the classifications of governments.

Moulton, John Fletcher (1844–1921): English mathematician and weapons adviser for the British war effort during the First World War.

Muhlenberg, Peter (1746–1807): Revolutionary soldier in the Continental Army; he became both a representative and a senator for Pennsylvania.

Mussolini, Benito (1883–1945): Italian political leader credited with the creation of fascism. He implemented a terrorist police state in Italy after a coup in October 1922. Mussolini led Italy into the Second World War by declaring war on both France and Great Britain in 1940.

Ortega y Gasset, José (1883–1955): Spanish liberal philosopher and essayist who advocated perspectivism while the Spanish government transitioned between monarchy, republicanism, and dictatorship.

Paine, Thomas (1737–1809): American revolutionary and author of the influential *Common Sense*. His prorevolutionary propaganda pamphlets were instrumental in spurring the colonists to declare independence from the Crown.

Pascal, Blaise (1623–1662): French mathematician and inventor of the mechanical calculator. He converted to Catholicism late in life, abandoning his scientific work and pursuing theology.

Paul, Randolph (1890–1956): Credited with creating the modern tax system, including the Internal Revenue Code, he served as the director of the Federal Reserve Bank of New York.

Penn, William (1644–1718): English philosopher and founder of the colony of Pennsylvania. He advocated religious freedom and democracy in colonial America.

Pericles (495– 429 BCE): Greek statesman and general of Athens during the Peloponnesian War. He is most famous for his written history of the war and his commentary on the war's revelation of human nature.

Pétain, Philippe (1856–1951): French general made famous for his outstanding leadership during the Battle at Verdun (World War I). He was appointed the premier of France during World War II, and his government quickly set up an authoritarian regime.

Peterson, Wilfred (1893–1954): Senior officer in the Royal Navy. He participated in the naval battle that sank the German battleship *Bismarck*.

Pius XII, Pope (1876–1958): Head of the Roman Catholic Church from 1939 until his death. He was a staunch opponent of communism and contributed to the rebuilding of Europe after World War II. Historians continue to debate whether he responded appropriately to the Holocaust.

Rauschenbusch, Reverend Walter (1861–1918): Christian theologian and Baptist minister who played a key role in the American Social Gospel movement.

Read, Leonard (1898–1983): founder of the Foundation for Economic Education, the first modern American libertarian think tank. Ayn Rand was an important adviser of his.

Rogers, Will (1879–1935): American cowboy, humorist, and actor who often provided political and social commentary. He was one of the best-known celebrities of the 1920s and 1930s, and he was beloved by the American people until his death in an airplane crash.

Roosevelt, Franklin (1882–1945): Thirty-second president of the United States. Along with Winston Churchill and Joseph Stalin, led the Allied Powers against Germany and Japan in World War II. He was the only American president ever elected to more than two terms, and his domestic politics revolved around resuscitating the country's ailing economy.

Seneca, Lucius (c. 3 BCE–65 CE): Tutor and adviser to the emperor Nero. He was a Roman Stoic philosopher and dramatist from the Silver Age of Latin literature.

Shaw, George Bernard (1856–1950): Irish playwright and cofounder of the London School of Economics. He wrote over sixty plays, most of which dealt with social problems. He was very concerned with the exploitation of the working class and remained a staunch socialist until his death.

Slichter, Sumner (1892–1959): Famous labor economist of the 1940s and 1950s. His was the standard economics textbook in America before 1950, and he informally advised President Harry Truman.

Smith, Adam (1723–1790): Key figure of the Scottish Enlightenment, he was the author of the first modern work of economics, *The Wealth of Nations*. He is widely known for pioneering modern capitalism, as well as for his moral philosophies.

Solzhenitsyn, Aleksandr (1918–2008): Russian and Soviet novelist who helped make the world aware of the Soviet Union's forced labor camps through his writings.

Sorensen, Theodore (1928–2010): President John F. Kennedy's special counsel, adviser, and speechwriter. He drafted much of Kennedy's Cold War correspondence and influenced foreign policy.

Spencer, Herbert (1820–1903): English philosopher and sociologist of the Victorian era. He wrote *Principles of Biology*, wherein he coined the term and concept "survival of the fittest."

Stalin, Joseph (1879–1953): Dictator of the Soviet Union from 1924 until his death. He fostered a cult of personality around himself and launched a command economy. He was also responsible for the Great Purge, a campaign to exterminate dissidents in the Communist party.

Sun Tzu (544–496 BC): Chinese philosopher, military general, and strategist who is believed to have been the author of the famous military strategy book *The Art of War*.

Thomas, Norman (1884–1968): American socialist and pacifist who was a six-time presidential candidate for the Socialist Party of America.

Tocqueville, Alexis de (1805–1859): French political thinker and historian known for his work on social conditions in western society. He wrote *Democracy in America*.

Toynbee, Arnold Joseph (1889–1975): British historian who wrote a popular twelve-volume analysis of civilizations. In the early twentieth century, he was a prominent consultant to the English government on international affairs, particularly in the Middle East.

Tytler, Alexander Fraser (1747–1813): British lawyer and writer who wrote cynically of democracies during his time as a professor in Scotland.

Webster, Daniel (1782–1852): American statesman during the antebellum period. He was Andrew Jackson's conservative counterpart, and he served in the House and the Senate before becoming secretary of state under three presidents.

Williams, Jack (1909–1998): Thirteenth governor of

Arizona. He was a political conservative, mayor of Phoenix, radio announcer, and advertising writer.

Willkie, Wendell (1892–1944): Dark-horse Republican Party nominee in the 1940 presidential election. He lost to Franklin D. Roosevelt and subsequently became the president's ambassador-at-large.

Wilson, Woodrow (1856–1924): Twenty-eighth president of the United States. A leader of the Progressive movement, he led the United States in the First World War and later promoted his plan for the League of Nations. He was known for his idealistic internationalism, calling for the United States to fight for democracy abroad.

Winthrop, John (1588–1649): Wealthy Puritan who obtained a royal charter from King Charles I to lead a group of fellow Englishmen and Englishwomen to the New World. He was elected governor of the Massachusetts Bay Colony in 1629.

Wolfe, Thomas (1900–1938): Master of autobiographical fiction. He wrote four lengthy novels and many short stories, most of which reflect on American mores and culture of the time. He is said to have influenced authors Jack Kerouac, Ray Bradbury, and Philip Roth.

Wormser, Rene A. (1896–1981): Counsel for a congressional committee commissioned to investigate tax-exempt foundations that were allegedly working—through education, government, and media—to turn America into a socialist nation.

ACKNOWLEDGMENTS

With thanks to my wife, Anne Brinkley; and my assistant, Sara Haji, of Austin, Texas.

To John Heubusch, who took the time to share his thoughts. To Nancy Reagan. To my friends Bob Barnett, Tim Duggan, Jonathan Burnham, Fred Ryan, and Joanne Drake.

And to James A. Baker III, a great source of wisdom, for all the encouragement.

—Douglas Brinkley

INDEX

INDEX

INDEX

INDEX

INDEX

INDEX

The money is coming from."

ON - SOFT ON CRIME

"You are sentenced to prison as long as it's made comfortable for you & your desire to remain. In checking out let the warden know, so he will know how many there will be for supper."

ON TAX

"Even when you make out a tax return on the level you don't know if you are a crook or a martyr."

LAWYERS

"Every time a lawyer writes something, he is not writing for posterity. He's writing so endless others of his craft can make a living out of trying to figure out what he said. Course perhaps he hadn't really said anything, that's what makes it hard to explain."

"The min. you read something & you can't understand it, you can be sure it was written by a lawyer. Then if you give it to another lawyer to read & he don't know just what it means then you can be sure it was drawn up by a lawyer. If it's in a few words and is plain & understandable only one way it was written by a non-lawyer."

POEM.

"The snow was blowing out of doors - the drifts were piling high, and I could see pedestrians as they were passing by. The faces of my Irish friends came dimly through the glass, as they trudged the icy streets to worship at their mass. I watched a while, went back to bed and cradled safe & sound as they braved those icy blasts on a sacred duty bound. I envy them their strength of heart, the faith that they revere, but on an ice cold Sunday morn it's good to be a Jew."

POEM "TCHR." CLARK MOLLENHOFF

"You are the moulders of their dreams - the gods who build or crush their young beliefs of Rt. or Wrong. You are the spark that sets afire the poet's hand or lights the flame of some great singer's song. You are the star of the young - the very young. You are the guardians of a million dreams. Your every smile or frown can heal or pierce a heart. Yours are a 100 lives - a 1000 lives. Yours the pride of loving them, the sorrow too. Your patient work, your touch make you the star of hope - that fills their souls with dreams - to make those dreams come true."

LORD MOULTON

"True civilization is measured by the extent of obedience to the unenforceable."